AMER
POPU
HISTORy AND
CULTURE

edited by

JEROME NADELHAFT

WRITING THE PUBLIC IN CYBERSPACE

REDEFINING INCLUSION ON THE NET

ANN TRAVERS

Routledge
Taylor & Francis Group

NEW YORK AND LONDON

First published 2000 by Garland Publishing, Inc.

This edition published 2015 by Routledge
711 Third Avenue, New York, NY 10017, USA
2 Park Square, Milton Park, Abingdon, Oxon OX14 4RN

First issued in paperback 2016

Routledge is an imprint of the Taylor & Francis Group, an informa business

Library of Congress Cataloging-in-Publication data is available from the
Library of Congress.

Writing the public in cyberspace : redefining
  inclusion on the net / by Ann Travers

ISBN: 9780815332657 (hbk)
ISBN: 9781138883413 (pbk)

To Elaine, Charlie, Jack and the students of SA 292:
for giving life to my questions.

Acknowledgments

In spite of the individualistic construction of authorship and the often solitary and seemingly endless hard work that goes into a work of this length, no one really writes anything alone. I am no exception as many family members, friends, colleagues and students contributed to the process. My early work on gender, public space and technology received professional support from Linda Fuller, Joan Acker, Greg McLauchlan and Linda Kintz at the University of Oregon and Mary Bryson, David Robitaille and Nancy Sheehan at the Faculty of Education at the University of British Columbia. Fiona Griffin, Fatima Correia, and Dad and Irene provided both practical and emotional support at crucial times. Michael Shepard and Peter Royce cheerfully helped me negotiate the complexities of the internet and computer technologies. Shauna Butterwick shared key resources with me at just the right time as she always seems to do. The Department of Sociology and Anthropology at Simon Fraser University supported the establishment of a course on information technology and society, thus giving me a chance to try out some of the ideas that emerged in the writing of this book. And the students of SA-292 shared their enthusiasm and insight with me as we explored public possibilities of cyberspace and in our classroom/lab. Thanks also to Thembisa Waetjen, Valerie Overgaard, Mary Tuominen, Jill Trotter, Luis Feijoo, and my brother and sister-in-law James and Anne Travers for cheering me on. And thanks to Charlie and Jack for keeping me company and Barbara for being Jack's best friend. The last word, at least in this instance, goes to Elaine Decker. In addition to being the best editor I could hope to find, her companionship and persistent faith in me made what was often a lonely endeavour considerably less so.

Contents

WRITING THE PUBLIC IN CYBERSPACE

REDEFINING INCLUSION ON THE NET

CHAPTER 1

Promises, Promises, Promises

In keeping with patterns of dissemination of new technologies, a utopian vision is part of the process of introduction. Historically, unqualified enthusiasm has ushered in technological change. It is not until we find ourselves virtually enslaved to technologies (Mander cites the examples of the automobile and the telephone)[1] that we start to identify the wide range of implications, intended and unintended, associated with their use. The business of spreading promises about information technology and internet connectivity has been taken up by private and public interests alike. Ushering in this technological change are promises of expanded democratic possibilities through the construction of truly inclusive public spaces.

The promise that computer-based communications technologies are creating a new, and at last a truly public space where all may participate equally regardless of gender, race, class (and sometimes even sexual orientation depending on who is doing the promising) is the focus of this book. This promise about the democratic potential of cyberspace has two key components. First, there is the promise that the technologies and the social spaces they foster are neutral, that is, they provide a forum where excluded identities can at last enjoy representation. Second, is the promise that universal access to the technologies and the related social spaces is both possible and desirable. I use a feminist/sociological perspective to examine critically these promotional promises.

THE PROMISE OF NEUTRALITY

Some cyberspace proponents promise that cyberspace provides a medium where gender, race, class, sexual orientation, (dis)ability are no longer operative in creating divisions relating to degrees of access and inclusion.

> Electronic notes, posted in group discussions, differ from hand- or type-written letters in several significant ways. Like public bathroom graffiti, their authors are sometimes anonymous, often pseudonymous, and almost always strangers. Which is the upside of incorporeal inter-action: a technologically enabled, postmulticultural vision of identity disengaged from gender, ethnicity, and other problematic construc-tions. On line, users can float free of biological and sociocultural deter-minants, at least to the degree that their idiosyncratic language usage does not mark them as white, black, college-educated, a high-school dropout, and so on.[2]

It is commonly argued that the anonymity of participation on the net makes it more democratic than other social spaces. Some authors, such as Michael Heim, insist that this very anonymity makes for a particularly inclusive space because individuals are free from the identifying charac-teristics targeted for discrimination. Heim exults that "We are more equal on the net because we can either ignore or create the body that appears in cyberspace."[3]

Tony Bates makes a similar point in heralding the advantages of computer-based communications technologies in educational settings. According to Bates,

> Because gender, race, physical appearance, status, or experience are not readily apparent, and because access to conferences can be made available to students and teachers alike, everyone participating is judged solely on the value of their contributions (although this is heav-ily dependent on the approach adopted by the tutor or moderator).[4]

Computer-based communications technologies may be facilitating the formation of many new communities. As Michael Benedikt observes,

> We are contemplating the arising shape of a new world, a world that must, in a multitude of ways, begin, at least as both an extension and a transcription of the world as we know it and have built it thus far.[5]

An evaluation of these celebratory claims is necessary to determine if these new communities are merely electronic clones of the world as we know it and have built it thus far.

THE MYTH OF NEUTRALITY

Far from being neutral artifacts and physical practices from which one can "float free", technologies are constructed in social contexts. In *The Real World of Technology*, Ursula Franklin makes a crucial distinction between prescriptive technologies that institutionalize hierarchical production processes and holistic technologies that reflect cooperative assumptions.[6] This distinction reminds us, too, that technologies must be understood as social practices that are hence constitutive of society and culture as much as constituted by them. Stone insists, indeed, that "technology and culture constitute each other."[7]

Technologies are developed within specific historical and cultural contexts and are interpreted and experienced within the context of specific power relations.[8] Technologies - defined as knowledge, practices, and artifacts[9] - emerge from social, political, and economic contexts and reflect specific relations of power in and of themselves. As Penley and Ross remark,

> cultural technologies are far from neutral and . . . they are the result of social processes and power relations. Like all technologies, they are ultimately developed in the interests of industrial and corporate profits and seldom in the name of greater community participation or creative autonomy.[10]

A closer examination of these allegedly neutral technologies will reveal a masculinist bias in both design and implementation, an uneven distribution of power, and a damaging denial of the body. I will explore each of these in turn.

Masculinist Bias

Given the context of the development of computer-based communications technologies, its masculine bias is not surprising. While the possibilities for cyberspace communities are multiple, the historical and contemporary military-industrial leadership behind most research and development and the context of a gendered, raced and classed international division of labour privilege a hierarchical and techno-rational form of cyberspace[11]. This form of cyberspace amounts to a

> postindustrial work environment predicated on a new hardwired com-
> munications interface that provides a direct and total sensorial access
> to a parallel world of potential work spaces. This interface, which is a
> world removed from the indirect and limited access provided by older
> print-based paradigms of visual literacy (Gibson 1984: 170), mediates
> between the sensorial world of the organically human and a parallel
> virtual world of pure digitalized information.[12]

While exciting forms of cyberspace have emerged in opposition to those which are hegemonic and monopolistic, we nevertheless have to contend with the cultural imperatives that are implicated in the very technological foundations of electronic communities and in the technologically-mediated processes of participation in these spaces. Wajcman's observation is very important in this respect: "As with science, the very language of technology, its symbolism, is masculine."[13]

> Programming itself involves constant creation, interpretation, and re-
> interpretation of languages. To enter the discursive space of the pro-
> gram is to enter the space of a set of variables and operators to which
> the programmer assigns names. To enact the naming is simultan-
> eously to possess the power of, and to render harmless, the complex of
> desire and fear that charge the signifiers in such a discourse; to enact
> naming within the highly charged world of surfaces that is cyberspace
> is to appropriate the surfaces, to incorporate the surfaces into one's
> own. [14]

As Cynthia Cockburn and others have observed, the notion of femininity has been constructed historically in opposition to technological proficiency and empowerment.[15] Technologies and technical proficiency are identified with masculinity. New technologies tend to be introduced, both in the workplace and in the classroom, in ways that are consistent with existing patterns of gender stratification. Thus, while for professional men, word processing and computer know-how generally translate into greater efficiency and empowerment on the job, the pattern of restricting women to service-oriented labour has not been broken by their acquisition of word processing or computer skills.[16]

Feminist analyses of technologies have identified crucial ways in which women's subordination is reinforced and indeed re-created. Historical accounts document the ways in which women's technological proficiency is coded as non-skill and yet used as the basis for labour-market ghettoization and domestic exploitation. Male proficiency with technologies is coded as skill and rewarded accordingly. Much of the literature on gender and technology focuses on the denial to women of access to skills and technological proficiency.[17] But the relationship between gender and technology is more complex than that. A dynamic that continues to occur is that, for the most part, men experience technological proficiency if not as liberating then as empowering, while women often experience technological proficiency as limiting and even enslaving.[18] We have only to think of good typing skills as an impediment to women being taken seriously in the workplace to realize that technological proficiency can be as much of an obstacle as the lack thereof.

Sex-typed differences between use and control are identified in the literatures on gender and technology and on gender and learning. Men are associated with "hard" mastery (control-oriented); women are associated with "soft" mastery (task-oriented). Men control tools; women use them. Similarly, computers tend to be introduced to children in ways that follow existing gender patterns. Computers are often introduced into schools in association with already male-identified fields such as mathematics and science rather than with language, an area where girls excel more quickly than boys in the early grades.[19]

Traditional theories of learning have located these differences in sex-typed cognitive styles. Sherry Turkle, for example, argues that these learning styles are actually complementary but that in our culture hard mastery is privileged over soft mastery.[20] Wajcman and others reject this individualistic model, arguing instead for a sociological or sociocultural rather than a psychological approach to learning. The classical individualistic theory where "it is the individual mind that acquires mastery over processes of reasoning and description, by internalizing and manipulating structures"[21] is giving way to a sociocultural understanding of thinking and learning.

> In contrast with learning as internalization, learning as increasing participation in communities of practice concerns the whole person acting in the world. Conceiving of learning in terms of participation focuses attention on ways in which it is an evolving, continuously renewed set of relations: this is, of course, consistent with a relational view, of persons, their actions, and the world, typical of a theory of social practice.[22]

The unit of analysis therefore shifts from the individual to the community. This awareness of the sociocultural construction of technologies and the cultures of electronic communities is an important tool for feminist analysis of cyberspace. Furthermore, viewing learning as a "collective, social process,"[23] which shifts attention away from individual difference to the sociocultural process of producing and reproducing knowledge is useful as we explore educational opportunities related to technologies.

Technology and Power

Computers, as with all technologies that reward proficiency with power, are identified as part of the "male" domain. Even within the computing counterculture, the so-called rebels are highly masculinist. Obsessed with the control of technology and dismissive of their physical beings, hackers are predominantly white, male and middle-class.[24]

Sally Hacker emphasized the connection between eroticism and technology and hence power and technology as a way of understanding how relations of power are built into technological products and processes. Before her death, Hacker embarked upon a groundbreaking analysis of this parallel: "Technology involves a strong sensual and erotic dimension. Whoever captures and defines erotic energy, a source of great social power, has more than an edge on the rest."[25] Hacker argued that systems of authority are based on the control and shaping of erotic desire and that much of this is accomplished through constructing relationships to technologies. The eroticization of control, for men, and the equation of femininity with that which can be controlled, go hand in hand with a gendered division of labour.

Hacker pointed out that technology itself is gendered "and thus reflects differences in power between men and women." Such patterns of dominance over underlings and submission to authority have their parallels in eroticism as well. Hacker suggests that a society whose major forms of organization are hierarchical must capture and shape eroticism in similar authoritarian molds. Thus, both technology and eroticism shape each other and society, but also reflect dominant patterns of interaction within society.[26]

Technical proficiency is constructed as male and this proficiency is about the ability to create and "crack" programs - in short, to control the computer. Hacker further observed that

> Much of the definition of approved sexuality and technology has to do
> with power. Some would no doubt decide they knew what was best for

the rest of us - that, say, certain classes of people couldn't handle a particular technology. It is not difficult to imagine who must be morally offended if the working class, women, or the enlisted soldier gained skills in certain "command" technologies.[27]

Hacker emphasized the privileging of the control of sensuality, of physicality, and the denial of the body in male interaction with technology. This is entirely in keeping with the cyberpunk/hacker ethic of disregard of the body and the dismissal of the body as "meat."[28]

Disembodiment

The argument that lack of embodiment increases democracy needs to be confronted. The dualism between the mind and body that characterizes western culture has placed the body and those more closely associated with it - women, people of colour, animals - in disrepute. Elizabeth Spellman identifies this tradition of hatred of the body as "somataphobia" and cites its operation in the delegation of physical tasks to those more closely associated with the body. A key signature of elitism is freedom from such tasks.[29] What assumptions are we perpetuating by this celebration of lack of embodiment in cyberspace? Denial of the body has been a foundation of forms of social and political engineering that have cruelly ignored the concerns of those for whom this denial is not possible - women, children, the elderly, the poor. Exalting the denial of the body reinforces the current gendered, raced, and classed division of labour.

The place of the body in computing culture is negligent. The glamour boys of the culture - whether in "reality" or "fiction"[30] are hackers, whose dedication to their craft is typified by denial of their physicality. This occurs both in terms of physical appearance in the form of lack of attention to personal grooming and in the denial of the physical needs of the body through marathon sessions at the terminal.

The cybernaut seated before us, strapped into sensory input devices, appears to be, and is indeed, lost to the world. Suspended in computer space, the cybernaut leaves the prison of the body and emerges in a world of digital sensation.[31]

Hacker ethics are high productivity-oriented and are reminiscent of normative dualism and Calvinist denial of the flesh. Liberal humanism's dichotomy between mind and body seems to be institutionalized in the development of these new technologies. The long history of association of women and the body and their devaluation makes this central characteristic of computing culture and the emerging culture of cyberspace problematic from a feminist perspective.

Most graphically, and perhaps most extremely portrayed in non-feminist cyberpunk fiction, the heroes of cyberspace are macho and a great deal of their machismo is established through the denial of their embodiment and indeed, all aspects of their personalities save those corresponding to techno-rationality. It may seem beside the point to be referring to works of fiction to identify and analyze aspects of the culture of actual cyberspace environments. After all, the extensive virtual reality dimension of cyberspace described in cyberpunk novels has yet to be available outside of the labs with the exception of video-arcade style entertainment versions here and there.[32] But cyberpunk fiction reflects key values and tensions of the culture of cyberspace and indeed, the postmodern world where technology is far more incursive than ever could be imagined and where, increasingly, it makes little sense to attempt to isolate technology from humanity, wherever those lines might be drawn. In keeping with her case for problematizing all boundaries, Haraway states that "the boundary between social reality and science fiction is an optical illusion."[33] This is highly consistent with the postmodern characterization of theories and historical accounts as "stories."[34]

The negation of the body in hacking cultures is not resolved by the nominal inclusion of women. As Stone remarks,

> much of the work of cyberspace researchers . . . assumes that the human body is "meat" - obsolete, as soon as consciousness itself can be uploaded into the network . . . . Cyberspace developers foresee a time when they will be able to forget about the body. But it is important to remember that virtual community originates in, and must return to, the physical . . . . Even in the age of the technosocial subject, life is lived through bodies.[35]

Feminists need to find ways to ensure that this privileged male desire to escape from the body is thwarted.

Conversational Virtues

Among women on the net, the majority tend to be (white) academic professionals. Even these relatively privileged, powerful women report experiences of exclusion[36] indicating serious problems for public cyber-space's inclusive potential. As Dale Spender observes, the gender gap with regard to computers is substantial:

> The world of computers and their connections is increasingly the world of men: as more research is done in this new area and more find-ings are presented, the more damning is the evidence. Men have more computers, spend more time with them, and are the dominating pres-ence in cyberspace.[37]

This "dominating presence" is imposed on the space in particularly inhospitable ways. The majority of participants in computer facilitated public discussions are male. On mixed-gender boards, even on feminist topics, men clearly dominate both in terms of volume of participation and agenda-setting.[38] For women, these public spaces are often experi-enced as hostile or unwelcoming. Because topics of interest to women are either non-existent, or fail to survive, the spaces may also be experi-enced as irrelevant. As in face-to-face social interaction, men monopo-lize the space. Spender observes this parallel between the results of her research on face-to-face interaction where men take up considerably more conversational space than women do and her research on gendered interaction on the net.[39] A significant problem for women on mixed bul-letin boards is the experience of sexual harassment. Participation by women is often effectively discouraged in this way. It is important to in-terpret sexual harassment as not solely about male sexual behaviour to-wards women but as a gate-keeping device that limits the extent to which women are able to participate in social spaces, including cyberspace.[40]

In spite of the degree to which identity can be concealed or overtly constructed on the net, gender is usually the one marker that remains visi-ble. Usernames or userids typically reveal the gender of the person. It is true that on bulletin boards where usernames or userids can be made up at will that it is possible for computer cross-dressing to occur. However, re-search to date has indicated that behaviour on these boards remains gen-der specific, nonetheless. Participants self-identifying as women take up considerably less conversational space, are less assertive and less aggres-sive while participants self-identifying as men adopt gender-appropriate behaviour and dominate, both in terms of quantity and content.[41] It seems then, that computer cross-dressing cannot be interpreted as "gender-bending" a way of undermining the dualisms between men and women because conversational practices in cyberspace remain gender-associated.

Admission to the Community

Electronic bulletin boards, however community-oriented, cannot help but reflect the gendered technological culture of computing. Lave and Wenger describe the processes whereby newcomers to a community of practice become old-timers, citing the tension between the need of old-timers to reproduce their community by initiating newcomers while at the same time desiring to maintain their privileged status. Through a process they identify as *legitimate, peripheral participation*, Lave and Wenger argue that individuals learn to become full members of a community by participating in that community.[42] It is plausible and historically resonant, that the tension between old-timers and newcomers in electronic communities will be resolved by according some newcomers the opportunity to participate fully while limiting participation for others. At times in history, trade unions and craft organizations, for example, have restricted the acquisition of skills to white men. Participation in cyberspace may be limited in similar ways as *norms* of behaviour that privilege some participants are developed and enforced through associated *sanctions*.

Understanding computer technologies sociologically, that is, *as culture*, allows us to reject the notion of neutrality and to explore how power relations are part of the fabric of public spaces.

THE PROMISE OF UNIVERSAL ACCESS

The second element of cyber utopia is the anticipated appearance of a new public space, a truly inclusive space. The very meaning of this word "public" has been theoretically and historically contested. As Nancy Fraser emphasizes, "public spheres exist in historically specific locations,"[43] and there is much evidence that in western societies those specific locations have not been characterized by their inclusivity.

Don Mitchell explores the history of conceptions of public space in an article analyzing the political struggle for People's Park in Berkeley, California. Mitchell characterizes the conflict as one between populist activists seeking to maintain the Park as *unregulated* "public" space capable of providing a refuge for the homeless and space for political organizing of all kinds, and the University of California's efforts to *regulate* the Park in the form of controlled recreation and to ensure middle-class comfort. This conflict culminated in riots in August 1991.[44] This struggle over the meaning of "public" had significant material and ideological consequences and as such, is consistent with a long history of such struggles:

> As ideological constructions . . . ideals of the public sphere take on double importance. Their very articulation implies a notion of inclusiveness that becomes a rallying point for successive waves of political activity. Over time, such political activity has broadened definitions of "the public" to include, at least formally, women, people of color, and the propertyless (but not yet foreigners). In turn, redefinitions of citizenship accomplished through struggles for inclusion have reinforced the normative ideals incorporated in notions of public spheres and public spaces. By calling on the rhetoric of inclusion and interaction that the public sphere and public space are meant to represent, excluded groups have been able to argue for their *rights* as part of the active public. And each (partially) successful struggle for inclusion in "the public" conveys to other marginalized groups the importance of the ideal as a point of political struggle.[45]

Mitchell emphasizes, moreover, that active struggle to claim inclusion in public space, to create space in public, is crucial for social groups to achieve any kind of legitimate identity. Without finding a place in public, social groups are not "seen." As such, struggle for public space is a crucial task for social change movements.[46]

The normative impetus behind varied conceptions of the public sphere in western society is that it be inclusive. What feminist criticism has revealed so effectively is that the so-called universality that is intended to create this openness and inclusivity is actually based on hegemonic norms. People whose characteristics of identity lie outside the power structure participate effectively (if at all) only to the extent to which they are willing or able to bracket their particularity.[47] As Pateman emphasizes, the very power of liberalism's conception of the universal individual is predicated upon disembodiment. Embodiment would reveal that this so-called "neutral" individual is actually male.[48] Additional feminist scrutiny of this category has revealed a host of other physical characteristics (race, class, sexuality, etceteras) associated with this hegemonic body.[49]

In liberal-democratic discourse the ideal of the public sphere is defined by virtue of its impartiality and universality. Political discussion and debate about social issues occur here. Partiality and particularity are assigned to the private sphere. As participants in the public sphere are expected to be neutral, people identified as 'other' through intersecting gender, sexual, racial and class identities are excluded. Indeed, the exclusion of women's 'private' concerns prevents the exposure of male dominance in personal relationships with women. Not only women's 'particular' concerns are excluded from the public realm, however but women *as women* are excluded.[50] The openness of the liberal-democratic public sphere is illusory but has been a theoretically and historically powerful misnomer.

The traditional dissection of social life into public and private characteristic of normative dualism does more than just place limits on who is able to participate in the public sphere; it also supports norms of behaviour and associated sanctions with regard to appropriate forms of "public" expression. The liberal-democratic opposition between the rational and the irrational rules affectivity, passion and play out of public discourse.[51] In short, the semiotic range is sharply restricted and this restriction reveals the hostility of the public realm to the body and those unable to disassociate themselves from it. As mentioned above, Spellman identifies this hatred of the flesh, or 'somataphobia,' as a key principle of liberal humanist discourse and one which justifies hierarchy on the basis of freedom from physical labour.[52] Tied to this hatred of the flesh is the imposition on women and other groups associated with the body to remain outside of or invisible within the public sphere. As Dorothy Smith agues, this invisibility is a modern 'virtue': the more successful women are in their roles, the less visible both women and women's work are.[53]

It is important to note that "not public" is not necessarily equivalent to "private." This dichotomy is not helpful in providing a basis for my investigation of the public nature of cyberspace. Rather, it is the degree to which spaces in cyberspace can be said to be inclusive as opposed to exclusive that determines how genuinely public they are.

Feminists call upon public spaces to provide the inclusivity that liberal democratic public theorists claim but do not deliver. In order to be genuinely inclusive, people must be able to participate as diverse individuals rather than in accordance with universal norms. The history of the western public sphere is one in which inclusivity has been largely illusory.

Just as access to and participation within dominant public spaces historically has been restricted to an elite, there is evidence that cyberspace is itself an elite space. Without deliberate contestation, at both the broader levels that influence access and the more specific levels that influence participation, traditional relations of domination are likely to be replicated in these "new" social spaces.

Applying assumptions about the public sphere to cyberspace is an interesting and important exercise. Brian Loader's edited volume entitled "The Governance of Cyberspace" is a case in point. Loader describes the work in this volume as addressing

> the alleged transformations in power relationships between individuals, government and social institutions as they are emerging in what is becoming known as cyberspace: a computer-generated public domain that has no territorial boundaries, is controlled by no single authority, enables millions of people to communicate around the world and maybe encourages post-hierarchical control of populations.[54]

De Kerckhove, while highly optimistic about the social impact of new information technology, comments that the only public space remaining (in Western society we presume) is television. Television, according to De Kerckhove, is genuinely public because it is available in real time, as opposed to the fluidity in space and time of cyberspace – and therefore public in the sense that everyone, presumably, has access to the same thing at the same time.[55] Rather than the simultaneous access to a common experience referred to by De Kerckhove or the questions of authority and control that are the topic of Loader's work, I focus on the inclusive and exclusive properties of public sites in cyberspace.

THE MYTH OF ACCESS

Economic Limitations

The most obvious challenge to the democratizing potential of computer-based communications technologies is in terms of material access - to the hardware and software required for participation, the education required to make use of it, the information required to get on board, and importantly, the sense of entitlement required to produce public written statements and to take up social space. Recent data indicate that the information revolution has yet to reach the majority of the world's population. In 1995 it was estimated that 50 million individuals in 175 (of 191) countries around the world made use of the internet. And yet we may be surprised to know that only one person out of every ten has ever used a telephone. As of 1995 only one percent of the world's population had access to the internet, 9 out of 10 people have never used a telephone, only a fourth of the world's population can afford to buy books and Tokyo has three times as many telephone lines as all of Africa.[56] While knowledgeable hackers can obtain computer equipment at low cost,[57] for most, the introduction to "the computer age" requires a substantial investment of time and money.

Literacy

Although there are a number of aspects of access that are peculiar to cyberspace, such as access to the technology and the internet provider, many aspects of access are shared with other social spaces that self-describe as public. This book focuses primarily on text-based sites in cyberspace so literacy is a key aspect of access, but this aspect is also important in a variety of non-cybernetically supported public spaces - letters to the editor, for example. Literacy and the related element of voice are socioculturally distributed and reflective of relations of power in stratified societies such as our own. Gender, race, and class are significant variables influencing the extent to which one is able and willing to "speak" in public—any public. Because many sites in cyberspace are text-based, in these at least and perhaps until virtual reality technology is further developed and accessible, one must write in order to be read or "heard". The combination of literacy and voice limits both access to the space and meaningful participation.

Citing Jane Mansbridge, Fraser notes that "Even the language people use as they reason together usually favours one way of seeing things and discourages others."[58] Writing, as technology and social practice, has a long history of elitism. The denial of literacy to groups marginalized on the bases of gender, race, class and position in the international division of labour is well known. In spite of the historical development of a culture of mass literacy in the West, basic literacy eludes significant proportions of groups marginalized on the bases of race and class. More engaged literacy, that is, the will and desire to write as a form of participation in the politics and culture of society, is associated with a sense of entitlement that is ludicrously far from being widely distributed.

Access to computer-based public spheres on the basis of literacy needs to be understood partly in terms of socioculturally determined competence and partly in terms of the sense of entitlement that inspires certain groups of people to make public their written statements. Ferdman notes that "In a society tending toward homogeneity, it is easy to think of literacy simply in terms of specific skills and activities."[59] However, citing de Castell and Luke, Ferdman points out that literacy is meaningful only in the social context of particular communities.

> An illiterate person is someone who cannot access (or produce) texts that are seen as significant within a given culture. That same person, in another cultural context, may be classified as being quite literate.[60]

This observation has particular relevance for textual sites in cyberspace, given that textual literacy and the entitlement to voice that is socioculturally produced combine with computer literacy to enable a person to gain access to public cyberspace.

Computer literacy must be understood within the historical and sociocultural context within which computer technology and "mastery" of it has been produced. Most arguments for the public, that is, inclusive, potential of new computer-based communications technologies are based on a naive dismissal of the relations of power that construct and interact with technologies.

Nominal access to the public sphere does not amount to opportunities for meaningful participation. As Fraser comments,

> The question of open access can be reduced without remainder to the presence or absence of formal exclusions. It requires us to look also at the process of discursive interaction within formally inclusive public arenas . . . .[There are] informal impediments to participatory parity that can persist even after everyone is formally and legally licensed to participate.[61]

Participation

Let us return to issues of universality and embodiment as they relate to inclusive participation in cyberspace. Monique Wittig notes that unless contested, implicit norms operate in social spaces. Her signature example is that of heterosexuality as a norm that is implicit in western social contexts unless contested.[62] It is my belief that the equation of democracy with anonymity reflects the assumption that universality can be achieved in cyberspace where it could not be achieved in other social spaces. The suggestion seems to be that in cyberspace we can at last "succeed" in leaving the body behind.

Racism, it is argued, for example, does not stand in the way of an

Asian-North American man in cyberspace because you cannot tell, unless he deliberately provides this information about himself, that he is of Asian origin: his words stand on their own. My concern, however, is that the very notions of universality that persist affect the identity we ascribe to individuals who do not identify themselves as `other.' As Wittig points out, unless one deliberately marks oneself as queer, unless one "comes out," one is assumed to be "normal," that is, heterosexual.

Lesbian and gay identities in the less cybernetic social worlds are good parallels with a range of identities in cyberspace because it is possible and often necessary to conceal them for reasons of safety/access/participation. In spite of the fact that "we are everywhere," as lesbian and gay activists pointedly declare, if "we" do not "come out," then the power of our numbers and the challenge to assumed norms and stereotypes remains invisible. This is precisely the political rationale behind the emphasis on "coming out" in queer social movements. The operation of implicit norms of identity in off-line social contexts suggests that anonymity is not a condition that unproblematically provides for greater inclusion in on-line social contexts. If people do not contest the norms that exclude them, they participate only partially. Aspects of their identities remain "in the closet." They are merely "enjoying" the privilege accorded to some by not contesting the assumption that their silence means they match the underlying universals of the public sphere (white, male, heterosexual, able-bodied, etceteras.). As long as the terms of participation remain unchallenged, diversity fails to characterize participation in these spaces.

While Wittig focuses in this example on the assumption of neutrality ascribed to heterosexuality, many other authors have emphasized the construction of the body as identified *away* from racial norms of whiteness,[63] away from gendered norms of maleness,[64] such that the body itself for the universalized white, heterosexual able-bodied male is non-existent as a marker. This socially constructed unmarked identity is the mythic character of the neutrality claimed by promoters of cyberspace as the ultimate public space.

Climate

In an article concerning the debate over political correctness at many American universities, Hoover and Howard designate quality of dialogue as indicative of climate as it relates to opportunities for participation. Specifically, they distinguish between traditional and critical dialogue. Traditional dialogue is defined as being characterized by the tactic of argumentation, which emphasizes "naming the other," and attack-oriented communication aimed at preserving "truth."[65] This definition of traditional dialogue closely resembles the polemical style of exchange referred to in the language of cyberspace as "flaming."[66] Critical Dialogue, in contrast, is defined by the acceptance of a multiplicity of perspectives and the deliberate attempt to construct community and establish inclusive public space. Drawing inspiration from the work of Richard Rorty, the authors emphasize that critical dialogue:

> consists of committment to discussion, to understanding, to acceptance not necessarily of the position of the other, but of the right of the other to a position, all without fear of retribution or loss. Critical dialogue therefore provides the key to community formation. Critical dialogue raises questions, stimulates conflict, suggests alternatives, and ensures interaction among members.[67]

In contrast,

> Attack-oriented communication aimed at preserving "truth" results in dogmatic argumentation that stifles dialogue and demands acceptance of values and traditions without question.[68]

The extent to which critical as opposed to traditional dialogue occurs, especially with regard to controversial topics in cyberspace (and topics related to gender, race and sexual orientation seem *always* to fall within this category), provides an indication of the extent to which this space can be said to encourage participation and hence inclusivity.

As in real space, in cyberspace, conversations often become heated. Participation is affected by an attack-oriented form of communication called "flaming." Aggressive messages are referred to as "flames" and such heated exchanges are referred to as "flame wars"[69]:

> Perched on a tightwire between the reasoned deliberation of text and the emotional immediacy of conversation, on-line communication sets itself up for a fall that is constantly realized. Fooled by the cool surface of electronic text, people lob messages cast in aggressively forensic impersonality into the midst of this combustively personal medium, and the result, routinely, is . . . [a] flame war.[70]

Given the prevalence of flaming in cyberspace and the monopolization of conversational space and agenda-setting by dominant social groups, self-identifying as a member of a marginalized group can be either undesirable or dangerous. Cyberspace is also a medium for textual violence, as Julian Dibbel's account "A Rape in Cyberspace", published in Mark Dery's *Flame Wars*, reveals.[71] In this essay describing and analyzing an incident whereby one participant textually "raped" another in a MUD (multi-user domain whereby a number of individuals participate in the construction of both a "story" and a social context), Dibbel explores the way in which the assumption of mind/body dualism allows some to insist that textual violence is not "real". The very real trauma experienced by the recipient of this violence and many other members of the community reveals that this dualism is not "real" in any absolute sense.

The likelihood that "coming out" as "other" would leave one open to marginalization on the bulletin boards and hence that the boards simply reflect power relations in off-line social spaces needs to be taken seriously. Members of marginalized groups have often found that separate space from those who enjoy pre-eminence in general spheres is the only way to ensure that they have space within which to participate fully. We are reminded of Fraser's observations that multiple public spaces, including the dynamic presence of subaltern counterpublics, are more conducive to genuine democracy, that is, are more genuinely inclusive than public spaces portraying themselves as "general". This perspective, grounded historically, is far more compelling than the argument that anonymity (and hence the bracketing of particularity characteristic of liberal democratic conceptions of the public sphere), increases the democratic character of a social space. Ultimately, the problems and possibilities within cyberspace are reflective of relations of domination and resistance in other social spaces. Anonymity does not allow us to bypass these deeply rooted conflicts.

The masculine culture of computing contributes to the construction of social spaces that women (among others) find unwelcoming. As Dale Spender remarks,

> It is extraordinarily difficult for young women to know how to behave in the computer classrooms and when they are on-line. The dominance of men and of extreme macho-values ensures that any woman who does stay has to find her own means of accommodation with the brutalising nature of the medium as it has been structured.[72]

The introduction of "environmental" issues and climate studies on many university campuses in North America has added an important dimension to discussions of accessibility and inclusivity.[73] Technical access has been revealed to be but a first step in increasing the inclusivity of these institutions. Increasingly, the debate about access has been broadened to include sociocultural factors and institutional practices that limit meaningful participation. Sexism, racism, homophobia, sexual harassment and hegemonically constructed canons of knowledge actively exclude students and faculty from participation in these institutions. Such climate studies suggest useful indicators for investigating the extent of participation in public cyberspace.

THE SEARCH FOR PUBLIC SPACE

Lave and Wenger characterize learning as participation in communities of practice.[74] Research on the gendered nature of computing technologies suggests that in cyberspace, the category of participants Lave and Wenger refer to as "old-timers" are largely male, white and middle class.

> It is no surprise that young males, with their cultural bent - indeed mission - to master technologies, are today's computer hackers and so populate the on-line communities and newsgroups.[75]

The implications of this on the production and reproduction of the culture of cyberspace are likely to be significant.

Communities produce and reproduce themselves as those in power create boundaries between insiders and outsiders.[76] Given the history of the ways in which privileged males have restricted access to technical proficiency,[77] it is reasonable to expect that this tension will be at least partly resolved by restricting opportunities for "newcomers" to become old-timers. Accepted will be people whose markers of identity are constructed as similar to those of the dominant group. In other words, as in other social spheres, norms of behaviour for participation and the sanctions associated with the violation of these norms will be constructed and enforced to reproduce the privilege of the dominant voices. Whether intentionally or not, middle class white men are likely to share power with other middle class men by explicitly and implicitly constructing norms of behaviour that reflect their particular culture. Writing the "public" according to the assumption that the particular culture of the dominant group is "universal" has this effect.

> Many of the engineers currently debating the form and nature of cyberspace are the young turks of computer engineering, men in their late

teens and twenties, and they are preoccupied with the things with
which postpubescent men have always been preoccupied. This rather
steamy group will generate the codes and descriptors by which bodies
in cyberspace are represented.[78]

The underlying assumptions of those who develop codes and practices for cyberspace and for participation in cybernetic communities will
have significant consequences for the culture of these spaces, particularly in terms of relations of power.

The democratic potential of new communications needs to be explored, not in terms of the classical liberal conception of the public
sphere as universal, but in terms of a feminist conception of the public
sphere, based on the inclusion, rather than the exclusion, of identifying
characteristics and persons associated with physical or behavioural
markers of marginality. In challenging ahistorical pro-technology arguments that identify access in principle to public cyberspaces with democratic tendencies, a feminist perspective can highlight the ways in which
power relations are embedded and enforced.[79] An understanding of the
ways in which cyberspaces are socially constructed may make possible
the identification of instances of, and opportunities for, resistance to social practices that reinforce existing patterns of domination. Ultimately,
such an analysis will inform theorizing about possibilities for inclusive,
and hence genuinely public spaces.

I engaged in this research not simply to justify a thesis that so-called
"public" cyberspaces are public only in the most narrow, formal sense of
the term, but rather to make visible the informal impediments to participation so that strategies for overcoming these impediments might more
successfully be devised and implemented.

Penley and Ross argue that this very investment in cyberspace by
feminists and leftists is crucial, contextualizing their arguments in an
awareness of what Heather Menzies refers to as "the information highway as restructuring agent."[80] While acknowledging that "the odds are
firmly stacked against the efforts of those committed to creating technological countercultures,"[81] they argue that there is a "pressing need
for more, rather than less, technoliteracy - a crucial requirement not just
for purposes of postmodern survival but also for the task of decolonizing, demonopolizing, and democratizing social communication."[82]
Nevertheless, while exploring public sites in cyberspace, attention
should be paid to the voices of feminist critics who warn of the ways in
which these spaces foster the disembodiment underlying western phi-

losophy. The absence of the semiotic in traditional liberal conceptions of the public sphere so strenuously objected to by Iris Young, for one,[83] seems to be taken to new extremes in a social space constructed exclusively by text.

Research on the social spaces fostered by computer-based communications technologies is emerging as a significant academic activity.[84] Important links between existing disciplines and this new context are being made, for example, in the fields of architecture, geography, sociology, communications, and women's studies. In addition, considerable research and writing is occurring on issues of regulation and censorship. To date, an investigation of a public site in cyberspace, driven by feminist insights about the way the "public sphere" historically and currently excludes much of the population, has yet to be undertaken. Because little is known about the long term social, economic, political and environmental consequences of new technologies, it is crucial that feminists engage with cyberspace as it is in the process of "becoming." The rapidity of technological change and its sociocultural consequence create the impression that it is not possible to understand this new medium. Its very fluidity makes it elusive. But feminists and critical researchers can, and should undertake case studies of specific sites. This very fluid medium can be "frozen," however briefly, and patterns of social interaction can be identified and analyzed.

In this book I relate my study of the public discussion area, *ncf.general*, of North America's second largest FreeNet, the National Capital FreeNet based in Ottawa, Canada, because it is deliberately constructed as a "public sphere" and because the commitment to "public access" to new technologies and information forms the basis of the FreeNet social movement. I begin my account of *ncf.general* in the following chapter.

NOTES

[1] Jerry Mander, *In the Absence of the Sacred: The Failure of Technology and the Survival of the Indian Nations*. (San Francisco: Sierra Club Books, 1991).

[2] Mark Dery. "Flame Wars," in *Flame Wars: The Discourse of Cyberculture*. Mark Dery, ed. (Durham and London: Duke University Press, 1994), p. 3.

[3] Michael Heim, "The Erotic Ontology of Cyberspace," in *Cyberspace: First Steps*, Michael Benedikt, ed. (Cambridge, Massachusetts: M.I.T. Press, 1992), p. 72.

[4] A.W. (Tony) Bates, *Technology, Open Learning and Distance Education*. (London and New York: Routledge, 1995).

⁵ Michael Benedikt, "Introduction," in *Cyberspace: First Steps*, Michael Benedikt, ed. (Cambridge, Massachusetts: M.I.T. Press, 1992), p. 23.

⁶ Ursula Franklin, *The Real World of Technology*. (Concord, Ontario: House of Anansi Press, 1990).

⁷ Alluquerre Rosanne Stone, "Will the Real Body Please Stand Up? Boundary Stories About Virtual Cultures," in *Cyberspace: First Steps*, Michael Benedikt, ed. (Cambridge, Massachusetts: M.I.T. Press, 1992).

⁸ Constance Penley and Andrew Ross, eds, *Technoculture*. (Minneapolis: University of Minnesota Press, 1991); Judy Wajcman. *Feminism Confronts Technology*. (University Park, PA: Pennsylvania State University, 1991).

⁹ Ursula Franklin, *The Real World of Technology*. (Concord, Ontario: House of Anansi Press, 1990).

¹⁰ Constance Penley and Andrew Ross, eds. *Technoculture*. (Minneapolis: University of Minnesota Press, 1991), p. xii.

¹¹ Heather Menzies, *Whose Brave new World? The Information Highway and the New Economy*, (Toronto: Between the Lines: 1996).

¹² David Tomas, "Old Rituals for New Space: Rites de Passage and William Gibson's Cultural Model of Cyberspace," in *Cyberspace: First Steps*, Michael Benedikt, ed. (Cambridge, Massachusetts: M.I.T. Press, 1992), p. 35.

¹³ Judy Wajcman, *Feminism Confronts Technology*.(University Park, PA: Pennsylvania State University, 1991).

¹⁴Alluquerre Rosanne Stone, "Will the Real Body Please Stand Up? Boundary Stories About Virtual Cultures" in *Cyberspace: First Steps*, Michael Benedikt, ed. (Cambridge, Massachusetts: M.I.T. Press, 1992), p. 109.

¹⁵ Cynthia Cockburn, *Machinery of Dominance: Women, Men and Technical Know-How*. (London: Pluto Press, 1985).

¹⁶ Heather Menzies, *Whose Brave New World? The Information Highway and the New Economy*. (Toronto: Between the Lines, 1996).

¹⁷ Cynthia Cockburn, *Machinery of Dominance: Women, Men and Technical Know-How*. (London: Pluto Press, 1985); Judy Wajcman. *Feminism Confronts Technology*. (University Park, PA: Pennsylvania State University, 1991).

¹⁸ While there is no doubt that assembly line production is as soul- and body-destroying for men as it is for women, technical competence as empowering has been more defining for male workers than for female. (Cynthia Cockburn, *Machinery of Dominance: Women, Men and Technical Know-How*. (London: Pluto Press, 1985).

¹⁹ Judy Wajcman, *Feminism Confronts Technology*. (University Park, PA: Pennsylvania State University, 1991); Jennifer S. Light. "The Digital Landscape: New Space for Women?" in *Gender, Place and Culture*, Vol. 2, No. 2, 1995, pp. 133-146.

20 Judy Wajcman, *Feminism Confronts Technology.* (University Park, PA: Pennsylvania State University, 1991), p. 156.

21 William F.Hanks, "Foreword" in *Situated Learning: Legitimate Peripheral Participation.* Jean and Etienne Wenger. (Cambridge: Cambridge University Press, 1991), p. 15.

22 Jean Lave and Etienne Wenger, *Situated Learning: Legitimate Peripheral Participation.* (Cambridge: Cambridge University Press, 1991), pp. 49-50.

23 Judy Wajcman, *Feminism Confronts Technology.* (University Park, PA: Pennsylvania State University, 1991), p. 157.

24 Katie Hafner and John Markoff, *Cyberpunk: Outlaws and Hackers on the Computer Frontier.* (New York: Simon and Schuster, 1991).

25 Sally Hacker, *Pleasure, Power and Technology: Some Tales of Gender, Engineering, and the Cooperative Workplace.* (Boston: Unwin Hyman, 1989), p. xvi.

26 Sally Hacker, *Pleasure, Power and Technology: Some Tales of Gender, Engineering, and the Cooperative Workplace.* (Boston: Unwin Hyman, 1989), p. 48.

27 Sally Hacker, *Pleasure, Power and Technology: Some Tales of Gender, Engineering, and the Cooperative Workplace.* (Boston: Unwin Hyman, 1989), p. 52.

28 William Gibson, *Neuromancer.* (New York: Ace Books, 1984).

29 Elizabeth Spellman, *Inessential Woman.* (Boston: Beacon Press, 1988).

30 A distinction that Donna Haraway disputes in her discussion of science fiction in *Simians, Cyborgs, and Women: The Reinvention of Nature.* (New York: Routledge, 1991).

31 Michael Heim, "The Erotic Ontology of Cyberspace," in *Cyberspace: First Steps*, Michael Benedikt, ed., (Cambridge, Massachusetts: M.I.T. Press, 1992), p. 64.

32 Howard Rheingold, *Virtual Reality.* (New York: Simon and Schuster, 1991).

33 Donna Haraway, *Simians, Cyborgs, and Women: The Reinvention of Nature.* (New York: Routledge, 1991), p. 149.

34 Judith Butler, *Gender Trouble: Feminism and the Subversion of Identity.* (New York: Routledge, 1990).

35 Allucquerre Rosanne Stone, "Will the Real Body Please Stand Up?: Boundary Stories About Virtual Cultures," in *Cyberspace: First Steps*, Michael Benedikt, ed. (Cambridge, Massachusetts: M.I.T. Press, 1992), p. 113.

36 Susan Herring, "Gender and Democracy in Computer-Mediated Communication," *Electronic Journal of Communication*; Dale Spender. "Electronic Scholarship: Perform or Perish," in *Women, Information Technology and Scholarship,*

Cheris Kramarae and Maureen Ebben, eds. (Urbana, Illinois: Centre for Advanced Study, 1993); Dale Spender, *Nattering on the Net: Women, Power and Cyberspace*. (Toronto: Garamond Press, 1995).

[37] Dale Spender, *Nattering on the Net: Women, Power and Cyberspace*. (Toronto: Garamond Press, 1995), pp. 165-166.

[38] Susan Herring, "Gender and Democracy in Computer-Mediated Communication," in *Electronic Journal of Communication*, 1994, p. 3

[39] Dale Spender, "Electronic Scholarship: Perform or Perish," in *Women, Information Technology and Scholarship*, Cheris Kramarae and Maureen Ebben, eds. (Urbana, Illinois: Centre for Advanced Study, 1993).

[40] Dale Spender, *Nattering on the Net: Women, Power and Cyberspace*. (Toronto: Garamond Press, 1995).

[41] Allucquerre Rosanne Stone, "Will the Real Body Please Stand Up?: Boundary Stories About Virtual Cultures," in *Cyberspace: First Steps*, Michael Benedikt, ed. (Cambridge, Massachusetts: M.I.T. Press, 1992).

[42] Jean Lave and Etienne Wenger, *Situated Learning: Legitimate Peripheral Participation*. (Cambridge: Cambridge University Press, 1991).

[43] Nancy Fraser, "Rethinking the Public Sphere: A contribution to the Critique of Actually Existing Democracy, in *The Phantom Public Sphere*, Bruce Robbins, ed. (Minneapolis: University of Minnesota Press, 1993), p. 17.

[44] Don Mitchell, "The End of Public Space? People's Park, Definitions of the Public, and Democracy," in *Annals of the Association of American Geographers*, 85 (1), 1995, p. 125.

[45] Don Mitchell, "The End of Public Space? People's Park, Definitions of the Public, and Democracy," in *Annals of the Association of American Geographers*, 85 (1), 1995, p. 117.

[46] Don Mitchell, "The End of Public Space? People's Park, Definitions of the Public, and Democracy," in *Annals of the Association of American Geographers*, 85 (1), 1995, p. 115.

[47] Nancy Fraser, "Rethinking the Public Sphere: A contribution to the Critique of Actually Existing Democracy, in *The Phantom Public Sphere*, Bruce Robbins, ed. (Minneapolis: University of Minnesota Press, 1993).

[48] Carole Pateman, *The Disorder of Women*. (Cambridge: Polity Press, 1989).

[49] Nancy Fraser, "What's Critical About Critical Theory? The Case of Habermas and Gender," in *Feminism as Critique*, Seyla Benhabib and Drucilla Cornell, eds. (Cambridge: Polity Press, 1987).

[50] Carole Pateman, *The Disorder of Women*. Cambridge: Polity Press, 1989, p. 12.

[51] Iris Marion Young, "Impartiality and the Civic Public," in *Feminism as Critique*, Seyla Benhabib and Drucilla Cornell, eds. (Cambridge: Polity Press, 1987).

[52] Elizabeth Spellman, *Inessential Woman*. (Boston: Beacon Press, 1988).

[53] Dorothy E. Smith, *The Everyday World as Problematic: A Feminist Sociology*. (Boston: Northeastern University Press, 1987).

[54] Brian D. Loader. *The Governance of Cyberspace: Politics, Technology and Global Restructuring*. London and New York: Routledge, 1997, editor's precis.

[55] Derrick De Kerckhove. *Connected Intelligence: The Arrival of the Web Society*. Toronto: Somerville, 1997.

[56] Harold Orlands. "Potpourri," in *Change Magazine*. (November/December 1998, Volume 30, Number 6), p. 7.

[57] Katie Hafner and John Markoff, *Cyberpunk: Outlaws and Hackers on the Computer Frontier*. (New York: Simon and Schuster, 1991).

[58] Nancy Fraser, "Rethinking the Public Sphere: A contribution to the Critique of Actually Existing Democracy, in *The Phantom Public Sphere*, Bruce Robbins, ed. (Minneapolis: University of Minnesota Press, 1993), p. 11.

[59] Bernardo M Ferdman, "Literacy and Cultural Identity," *in Harvard Educational Review*, Vol. 60, No. 2, May 1990, p. 186.

[60] Bernardo M Ferdman, "Literacy and Cultural Identity," *in Harvard Educational Review*, Vol. 60, No. 2, May 1990, p. 187.

[61] Nancy Fraser, "Rethinking the Public Sphere: A contribution to the Critique of Actually Existing Democracy, in *The Phantom Public Sphere*, Bruce Robbins, ed. (Minneapolis: University of Minnesota Press, 1993), p. 10.

[62] As cited by Nancy Fraser in "Rethinking the Public Sphere: A contribution to the Critique of Actually Existing Democracy, in *The Phantom Public Sphere*, Bruce Robbins, ed. (Minneapolis: University of Minnesota Press, 1993).

[63] Audre Lorde. *Sister Outsider: Essays and Speeches*. (Trumansburg, N.Y: Crossing Press, 1984); Vron Ware. *Beyond the Pale: White Women, Racism and History*. (London: Verso, 1992).

[64] Elizabeth Spellman, *Inessential Woman*. (Boston: Beacon Press, 1988).

[65] Judith D. Hoover and Leigh Anne Howard, "The Political Correctness Controversy Revisited: Retreat from Argumentation and Reaffirmation of Critical Dialogue," in *American Behavioral Scientist*, Vol. 38, No. 7, June/July 1995.

[66] Mark Dery, *Flame Wars: The Discourse of Cyberculture*. (Durham and London: Duke University Press, 1994).

[67] Judith D. Hoover and Leigh Anne Howard, "The Political Correctness Controversy Revisited: Retreat from Argumentation and Reaffirmation of Critical Dialogue," in *American Behavioral Scientist*, Vol. 38, No. 7, June/July 1995, p. 971.

[68] Judith D. Hoover and Leigh Anne Howard, "The Political Correctness Controversy Revisited: Retreat from Argumentation and Reaffirmation of

Critical Dialogue," in *American Behavioral Scientist*, Vol. 38, No. 7, June/July 1995, p. 972.

[69] Mark Dery, "Flame Wars," in *Flame Wars: The Discourse of Cyberculture*. Mark Dery, ed. (Durham and London: Duke University Press, 1994).

[70] Julian Dibbel, "A Rape in Cyberspace; or, How an Evil Clown, a Haitian Trickster Spirit, Two Wizards, and a Cast of Dozens Turned a Database into a Society," in *Flame Wars: The Discourse of Cyberculture*, Mark Dery, ed. (Durham and London: Duke University Press, 1994), p. 261.

[71] Julian Dibbel, "A Rape in Cyberspace; or, How an Evil Clown, a Haitian Trickster Spirit, Two Wizards, and a Cast of Dozens Turned a Database into a Society," in *Flame Wars: The Discourse of Cyberculture*, Mark Dery, ed. (Durham and London: Duke University Press, 1994).

[72] Dale Spender, *Nattering on the Net: Women, Power and Cyberspace*. (Toronto: Garamond Press, 1995), p. 200.

[73] Roberta M. Hall and Bernice R. Sandler, *The Classroom Climate: A Chilly One for Women?* (Washington, D.C.: Project on the Status and Education of Women, Association of American Colleges: 1982), .p. 2.

[74] Jean Lave and Etienne Wenger, *Situated Learning: Legitimate Peripheral Participation*. (Cambridge: Cambridge University Press, 1991).

[75] Michael Benedikt, "Introduction," in *Cyberspace: First Steps*, Michael Benedikt, ed. (Cambridge, Massachusetts: M.I.T. Press, 1992), p. 6.

[76] Sneja Gunew and Anna Yeatman, eds. *Feminism and the Politics of Difference*. (Halifax, Nova Scotia: Fernwood Publishing, 1993).

[77] Cynthia Cockburn, *Machinery of Dominance: Women, Men and Technical Know-How*. (London: Pluto Press, 1985).

[78] Alluquerre Rosanne Stone, "Will the Real body Please Stand Up?: Boundary Stories About Virtual Cultures," in *Cyberspace: First Steps*, Michael Benedikt, ed. (Cambridge, Massachusetts: M.I.T. Press, 1992), pp. 103-104.

[79] Nancy Fraser, "Rethinking the Public Sphere: A contribution to the Critique of Actually Existing Democracy," in *The Phantom Public* Sphere, Bruce Robbins, ed. (Minneapolis: University of Minnesota Press, 1993).

[80] Heather Menzies, *Whose Brave New World? The Information Highway and the New Economy*. (Toronto: Between the Lines, 1996).

[81] Constance Penley and Andrew Ross, eds. *Technoculture*. (Minneapolis: University of Minnesota Press, 1991), p. xiii.

[82] Constance Penley and Andrew Ross, eds. *Technoculture*. (Minneapolis: University of Minnesota Press, 1991), p. xvi.

[83] Iris Young, "Impartiality and the Civic Public," in *Feminism as Critique*, Seyla Benhabib and Drucilla Cornell, eds. (Cambridge: Polity Press, 1987).

[84] Lynn Cherny and Elizabeth Reba Weiss, eds. *Wired Women: Gender and New Realities in Cyberspace.* (Seattle: Seal Press: 1996); Cheris Kramarae and Maureen Ebben, eds. *Women, Information Technology and Scholarship.* (Urbana, Illinois: Centre for Advanced Study, 1988); Heather Menzies. *Whose Brave New World? The Information Highway and the New Economy.* (Toronto: Between the Lines, 1996); Dale Spender. *Nattering on the Net: Women, Power and Cyberspace.* (Toronto: Garamond Press, 1995).

CHAPTER 2

Case Study of the National Capital Freenet

In 1995, I conducted a small study of a self-avowedly public text-based public discussion area on the Ottawa-based National Capital Freenet. This freenet provided internet access and social space to participants from the local area in Ottawa, Canada, beyond to North America and even featured some participation from other continents. As my purpose was to explore the inclusive nature of *ncf.general* rather than to examine the individual behaviors of contributors, I have changed all names and userids. I have treated the messages, or posts, as public declarations, that is as statements by individuals in a public arena. Spelling, grammar and sentence structure are reproduced as they were in the original messages.

A VISIT TO *NCF.GENERAL*

Sitting in front of my computer, I telnet in to the National Capital FreeNet by typing freenet.carlton.ca at the telnet prompt. I know I've made it when I see what appears to me to be a heavily armed space figure but which in fact is intended to be a digitalized Maple Leaf in honour of the site's Canadian physical location:

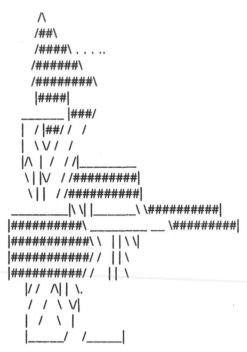

and the words:
Welcome to the National Capital FreeNet

About *ncf.general*

The Freenet movement originated in Cleveland, Ohio in 1986.[1] Freenets are committed to expanding public access to computer-based communications technologies and cyberspace.[2] *Ncf.general* is the public discussion area of North America's second largest FreeNet. Physically based in Ottawa, Canada and known widely as the "Ottawa FreeNet," this site in cyberspace was formally established in November 1991. The actual system became a part of public cyberspace on February 1, 1993. It self-describes as follows:

> The National Capital FreeNet is a computer based information service designed to meet the present information needs of the people and public agencies in the region, and to prepare the community for full and broadly based participation in rapidly changing communication environments.

The National Capital FreeNet is incorporated as a non-profit community utility that is free to everyone in the community, and will neither charge nor pay for any information or other services it provides.

The National Capital FreeNet is governed by an elected Board of Directors according to established by-laws.[3]

Some basic conditions of access have been satisfied by the National Capital FreeNet (NCF) and hence *ncf.general*. These concern access to technology and access to the site. NCF terminals are provided in a number of Ottawa public libraries. Technically, therefore, ownership of a computer is not a criterion for access and participation. Membership in NCF is free and open to anyone. Registration can be accomplished online or by filling out and returning a registration form that is available through the public library system.

I am asked to "login" while being informed that I may login as "guest." I am a registered user because I downloaded the NCF registration form and mailed it in. The only cost involved in this registration process was the price of a stamp.

I type in "as409," the user number assigned to me when I registered. I am asked for my password and I type that in as well: ******. Although we all logon by user number, whenever we post a message a name is displayed beside the number. Mine is simply "Ann Travers," but had I wanted to, I could have registered as "The Jolly Green Giant". Immediately after my password is accepted, I am informed that I have no mail. As I have rarely done more than lurk in this site, it is not a surprise.

I hit "return" to continue as instructed and my screen is filled with several public service announcements. In this case, I am reminded of the upcoming NCF on-line Annual General Meeting and I am encouraged to make a donation to NCF to enable it to purchase more phone lines. From what users say in their posts, using a modem (rather than the telnet connection I have access to through the University where I work) makes it really difficult to get on-line. The busy signal seems to be a common occurrence for NCF users who use a modem.

I hit return to reach the main menu which looks like this:

<<<The National Capital FreeNet—Main Menu>>>
1 About the National Capital FreeNet . . .
2 Administration . . .
3 Post Office . . .
4 Public Discussion . . .

5 Social Services, Health, & Environment Centre . . .
6 Community Associations . . .
7 The Government Centre . . .
8 Science, Engineering and Technology Centre . . .
9 Schools, Colleges and Universities . . .
10 The Newstand . . .
11 Libraries . . .
12 Special Interest Groups . . .
13 Communications Centre . . .
14 Professional Associations . . .
15 Help Desk . . .
16 Menu principal francais . . .
17 Make a donation to keep FreeNet free

h= Help, x=Exit FreeNet, p=previous, u=up, m=main
Your Choice==>

I type in "4" to reach the public discussion area. The menu for this area appears on my screen, as follows:

Public Discussion Menu (go public)

1 About the Public Discussion menu Read this before posting any-
thing!
2 General Bulletin Board (ncf.general)
3 Babillard general francophone (ncf.francais)
4 Help Desk - Questions and Answers (ncf.admin)
5 A big thank-you to our volunteers (ncf.admin.volunteer.thank-you)
6 Questions and Help with Modems and Communications . . .
7 NCF Policy Discussions and Resolutions . . .
8 Chat with Other Users . . .
9 Public Advisory Council on the Information Highway
10 Ottawa Area Buy and Sell Postings (ott.forsale)
11 Ottawa Area Housing Postings (ott.housing)
12 Ottawa Area Events Postings (ott.events)
13 Ottawa Area Jobs Postings (ott.jobs)

h= Help, x=Exit FreeNet, p=previous, u=up, m=main
Your Choice==>

I choose the general bulletin board *"ncf.general"* by typing in "2". The subject headings of the first 20 messages and the identity of the individuals who posted them are displayed on my screen. Following are the first twenty subject headings I saw on the day my research commenced, December 21, 1994.

Articles range from 21601 to 22687: ncf.general

** 21601. Holidays	Elizabeth W.
21602. Exp. Comp. Serv. Tech close to CNE seeks employment	Unev B.
21603. Re: Intel's Pentium Chip	Pete S.
34856. Re: No Quebecer As PM ! If Quebec Goes ?	Sylvia W.
21604. Re: Seasons Greetings	David D
21605. Re: GUNS,GUNS,OH GOD GUNS	Ricardo C
21606. Re: Holidays	!Dan R
21607. Re: NO! simply means NO!	Bert R
21608. Scary thought	Billy Z.
21609. Re: Seasons Greetings	Bert R
21610. Re: GUNS,GUNS,OH GOD GUNS	Bert R
21611. Re: NO! simply means NO!	Andrew J.
21612. reporter query	Nancy M
21613. Re: NO! simply means NO!	Gene A
21614. Re: Women being raped and murdered?	Suzanne M
21615. Re: Questions about Santa	Evan T
21616. Help a reporter	Julian D
21617. Re: Rosanne Skoke, Liberal MP	Steven P
21618. Re: Seasons Greetings	Jason V
21619. Re: Women being raped and murdered?	Jason V

h=HELP, q=quit, t=type(read), n=next, s=next w/same subj, c=contribute(post)
Enter Command:

I can scroll through all the subject headings for the more than 1,000 posts electronically "stored" in *ncf.general* at any given time. Or, I can simply type in the command "n" to begin reading the first few posts:

Article #21601 (22687 is last): Newsgroups: ncf.general From: ad110@FreeNet.Carleton.CA (Elizabeth W) Subject: Holidays Date: Wed Dec 21 10:17:24 1994 Because I plan to take a Christmas holiday, there won't be any more Findlay funnies, at least until mid January. Seasons greetings to one and all. - ad110@freenet.carleton.ca (Elizabeth W) -

End of File, Press RETURN to quit

Article #21602 (22687 is last): Newsgroups: ncf.general From: ah033@FreeNet.Carleton.CA (Unev B) Subject: Exp. Comp. Serv. Tech close to CNE seeks employment Reply-To: ah033@FreeNet.Carleton.CA (Unev B) Date: Wed Dec 21 10:50:14 1994 I am an experienced Computer Sevice Tehnician with a four years of knowledge of repair and installation of IBM Clones and its peripherals. I have good knowledge of many a popular softwares. I have installed and configured Netware 2.2 and 3.12. My salary expectation is only $11.00 hour. I am not under selling myself and this is all I wanted now. If interested, please call me at 247-9796 and leave a message if I cannot answer the phone personnaly. Unev.

Article #21603 (22687 is last): Newsgroups: ncf.general From: aa458@FreeNet.Carleton.CA (Pete S) Subject: Re: Intel's Pentium Chip Reply-To: aa458@FreeNet.Carleton.CA (Pete S) Date: Wed Dec 21 10:50:33 1994 In a previous posting, David D (av142@FreeNet.Carleton.CA) writes: Last night on the news, the had a story about students discovering a calculation using a whole number division problem that resulted in an error. Up until now, the Intel's Pentium chip had been claimed to only produce calculation errors to the 12th decimal place. I wanted to know, I didn't record down the calculation the students gave and I was wondering if anyone else saw the broadcast. Please email me if you did for the division problem. I believe there's information in the PC-Tech sig.— :

Here I stand at the crossroad's edge, : Afraid to reach out for eternity. - : One step, when I look down, - Queensyrche,: I see someone else not me. Promised Land

Article #21604 (22687 is last): Newsgroups: ncf.general From: aj918@FreeNet.Carleton.CA (David D) Subject: Re: Seasons Greetings. Date: Wed Dec 21 11:41:29 1994 In a previous article, bl737@FreeNet.Carleton.CA (Janice M) says: [You know who you are, I won't tell you your names, but guys I want to tell you that I hate you from the bottom of my heart and I wish you a terrible new year. Don't call me a man hater, because you are not men.] Janice, your honesty is admirable. However, my naievite forces me to dream that this is a season of good will towards man (and woman), so I wish that you would have waited until later to say something so vile. It is not very nice of you to defile the holiday spirit with your poison. I regret reading what you write, I hope I will be intelligent enough to ignore you in the future. I wish you a very happy new year and a very merry christmas, and I sincerely wish that 1995 will be a year of healing for you. Not only that, but I pray that the gods will bring you a good man who will make you happy and who will show you what love is like.

Article #21605 (22687 is last): Newsgroups: ncf.general From: as913@FreeNet.Carleton.CA (Ricardo C) Subject: Re: GUNS,GUNS,OH GOD GUNS Reply-To: as913@FreeNet.Carleton.CA (Ricardo C) Date: Wed Dec 21 13:25:48 1994 In a previous posting, Bert R (bc106 In a previous posting, Simon D (az088@FreeNet.Carleton.CA) writes: The difficulty with your argument which essentially blames violence for guns being readily available is that you may have to explain the situation in Switzerland. There, all males between 18-50 years of age are in the military and have at home their automatic rifle. Yet, the murder rate in the country is very low. The point is that in the US, something else besides the ready availability of guns is causing the carnage. Which is not to say that disarming Americans would not be a great idea, but don't expect that—even if it could be done—it would be successful in reducing the crime rate by very much. There is one major difference between the US and Switzerland. Every Swiss male is trained in proper use, care, and storage of weapons. The vast majority of Americans are not. 7mShown 88%, m —So, what you are saying then, is the reason that gun related crimes are so high in the States is because they don't have proper training? Ricardo.

Article #21606 (22687 is last): Newsgroups: ncf.general From: aa610@freenet5.carleton.ca (!Dan R NCFreeNet]) Subject: Re: Holidays Reply-To: aa610@FreeNet.Carleton.CA (!Dan R NCFreeNet]) Date: Wed Dec 21 13:37:05 1994 Mary F ad110@FreeNet.Carleton.CA wrote: Because I plan to take a Christmas holiday, there won't be any more Findlay funnies, at least until mid January. Seasons greetings to one and all. Thanks, Elizabeth! Happy Xmas! # # ## ## ###### ##### ##### # ###### # ## # ###### ##### # ## # ## ## ##### ##### ## ## # # # # ## # ###### # ## # # ##### 7mShown 54%, m # ## ###### # #### ##### # # ## ##### # ## # # # # ## ## ## ## ###### # # #### # # ## # # #### # # # ##### # # # # # ###### ## ## ## # # ## # # # ## ## # ##### # # # # # #### # # # # # ####—-IAN! !Dan R aa610@freenet.carleton.ca System Administrator Ottawa The National Capital FreeNet LiBert Rel de la Capitale nationale Canada

Article #21607 (22687 is last): Newsgroups: ncf.general From: bc106@FreeNet.Carleton.CA (Bert R) Subject: Re: NO! simply means NO! Reply-To: bc106@FreeNet.Carleton.CA (Bert R) Date: Wed Dec 21 13:44:26 1994 In a previous posting, Janice M (bl737@FreeNet.Carleton.CA) writes: In a previous article, bc106@FreeNet.Carleton.CA (Bert R) says: deleted] [I hate no one, you are accusing me of hatred because you don't like no one to question the privelage of male dominated society. Fighting for our equality is no hatred.] Janice, you have stated that "all men secretly desire to hurt women", that I didn't say they do. I said they have the potential, and the social conditioning to do that. Shall I trundle over the Fem SIG and quote the exact article in context ? 7mShown 23%, m men are to blame for all the problems of society, that things done to women by women are men's fault, that you hate Aubrey(!) because he is a Men are indeed behind most of society's problems. Have you seen a female pimp, a drug pusher, bank robber, rapist, war monger, mass murderer, all are men women are the victims men are the victimizers. Female pimp? I remember one woman back in Saint John who got two years for prostituting her teenage daughter. Female drug pusher? Yes. My roommate used to buy from one. Female bank robber? Never met a bank robber. Female rapist? How about those woman out west a few years back who stripped the guy who walked in on a stagette party? He was ridiculed for not enjoying the experience. Female war monger? Margaret Thatcher. Female mass murderer? Mrs. Smith of recent fame. Female sposal abuser? One in the last rooming house where I lived. She took advantage of the fact that her boyfriend would not hit her no matter what she did to him . 7mShown 51%, m Wake up to reality, Janice. man. I would suggest that you seek counselling. You are not rational. I am not irrational. I just tell you the facts that you hate, and I have nothing to apologize for. I hate? Little girl, I have had far more go wrong in my life than the one incident you have. I know the true meaning of hate. And you display it. You, child, are andryphobic. And before you start with the "you're a man, blah, blah, blah", I know what paranoid schizophrenia and irrationality sound like; I've been there. You maybe schizophrenic I am not. Go get help, maybe then you can be sane enough to see the truth of my arguments. Little one, I went through several years of therapy. I am sane. You, however, cannot admit that you might be wrong when everyone who answers you disagrees vehemently with you. I think it's fairly obvious to anyone who reads that you are a very bitter person. Quite likely you were a 7mShown 78%, m spoilt brat beforehand, who got ticked when mommy and daddy's money couldn't buy back your innocence. What's the matter, were you brought to reality once and couldn't handle it? There is nothing so beautiful as a woman at the peak of ecstasy. And nothing so satisfying as bringing her there, repeatedly. Another of your mysoginst desires to control women. So, bringing pleasure to a willing partner is misogynistic? You seem incapable of seeing beauty in life, Janice. My previous comment about you seeking help was meant as advice. This time, I'm saying: Get help you nut! Before you hurt someone.—

There is nothing so beautiful as a woman at the peak of ecstasy. And nothing so satisfying as bringing her there, repeatedly.

I notice that participants take pieces of each other's posts and present their responses in conversational form. This splicing of text is a form of social interaction suggestive of washroom graffiti but I suspect the extent of this practice is unique to text-based cyberspaces. Another feature I observe is that many participants end their messages with what is called a sig.file - a prepared message ranging from their names and email addresses to a personal statement to a quote from a favourite author or artist. These sig.files add another layer to the conversation in *ncf.general*.

WRITING THE PUBLIC IN CYBERSPACE

Ann Game remarks in *Undoing the Social*, that "the social is written."[4] Perhaps nowhere is this more apparent than in a text-based site in cyberspace. It is the act of writing itself that is required to render the construction and maintenance of the technical infrastructure a social space, rather than simply a software program. The extent to which this space is "public" is also partially determined by the act of writing. Three of the eight conversations selected for analysis in this book refer specifically to the "public" nature of cyberspace and/or *ncf.general*. These discussions, these writings of the public, reflect ways in which communities of practice, to use Lave and Wenger's terminology, construct themselves and both construct the sociocultural context and are constructed by it. How is the "public" nature of *ncf.general* constructed and/or contested, both ideologically, and in practice?

The restriction of data to that available on-line without solicitation by me as a researcher takes advantage of the unique opportunity available in cyberspace to study "spontaneous" social action. It is my contention that the social space of *ncf.general* is *written* through participation and that it is the text itself that constitutes social interaction. While a more exhaustive study might include data from interviews with participants, I am less concerned with determining the intention of participants in writing the public in cyberspace and more concerned with the effect of that writing in terms of the climate of *ncf.general*.

In studying the public discussion area of the National Capital Freenet, I use the following questions relating to access and participation as bookmarks:

* How is the public defined by participants?
* Does "freedom of speech" equal inclusivity/democracy?
* Does anonymity create greater inclusivity/democracy?

- Does the freedom to construct the personality make for a more inclusive space?
- How are the norms and sanctions of a particular space used to create insiders of some and outsiders of others?
- What forms of social control, or policing of the public space, are operative?

Having established the fundamentally elitist nature of cyberspace in my discussion of obvious limitations in Chapter One, my focus in this chapter is on specific inclusive and exclusive tendencies *within ncf.general*. I explore *ncf.general* as "public" cyberspace to identify ways in which access is available or limited, and to identify ways in which participation is encouraged or discouraged. In keeping with the definition of "public" as "inclusive", I explore issues of access and participation in *ncf.general* accordingly. In the end I hope to find out how genuinely public or inclusive this small piece of cyberspace is.

The data for this study consists of the almost 3,000 posts contributed to *ncf.general* over a two month period, beginning on December 21, 1994 and ending on February 20, 1995. Additional data is provided by official National Capital FreeNet documents relating to history, organization and by-laws, available on-line during the period of my research. I did not try to obtain figures on passive participation (referred to as "lurking"). My data is restricted to visible participation, in the form of posted messages.

In my analyses of *ncf.general* the variables relating to inclusive/exclusive tendencies I attend to are gender, race and sexual orientation. I operate, of course, with the understanding that these indicators of identity overlap and intersect.

Over the two month period of my research, topics of discussion in *ncf.general* include debates between smokers and non-smokers about smoking bans in public places, racism/white supremacy, sexual orientation, freedom of speech and political correctness, government policies on welfare and taxation, gun control, French language policies and violence against women. *Ncf.general* is also used as a site for dissemination of information with regard to local (Ottawa and surrounding area) issues and activities and as a place to solicit and share information with regard to computer technology. In my study of this site I identify informal impediments to participation and instances of more inclusive behaviour through textual analysis of a number of specific conversations or "threads." A "thread" refers, in "netspeak," to a discrete conversation on a more or less specific topic or topics.[5] I selected eight "threads" for detailed textual analysis. I have called them:

1. Frequent Posters
2. NCF.Board
3. Internet Racism
4. Violence Against Women - (Janice M)
5. Reform MP for Nanaimo-Cowichan
6. Racial Purity/White Supremacy (Ernie T)
7. Long Live Canada (Elliott D)
8. Bert R's Signoff

Each thread is named according to the principle topic(s) of discussion. The first three threads were selected because they explicitly or implicitly address *ncf.general* specifically or cyberspace more generally *as public space*. As such, they contain explicit or implicit discourses of the public and hence articulations of appropriate participatory behaviour. No additional threads of this nature were in evidence. It is these threads that are the focus of the remainder of this chapter. The final five threads exemplify the many conversations I found in *ncf.general* that addressed the traditional bases of exclusion from the public sphere that I focus on - gender, race and sexual orientation. There is no question that socioeconomic class is a key variable affecting both access to, and participation in, public spaces of all kinds and most certainly in public cyberspaces. Unlike race, gender and sexual orientation within *ncf.general*, class is a more amorphous and less specific form of identity, both as a topic of conversation and in terms of personal identity. Including class in my research focus would require an exhaustive study that employed methods for ascertaining personal information about participants, a study that is beyond the scope of this book and as yet without precedent in the literature on cyberspace

Text-based sites in cyberspace present unique challenges for qualitative research in that they contain "data" that conforms neither to traditional notions of text as document nor to the face-to-face social interaction that inspires ethnography. Traditional research methods make a distinction between spontaneous social interaction and historical document. The methods associated with document analysis[6] are not designed for an exclusively text-based community such as *ncf.general* and ethnographic methods assume participant observation in face-to-face settings[7]. As Ian Hodder emphasizes in a chapter entitled "The Interpretation of Documents and Material Culture," "What people say" is often very different from "what people do."[8] In *ncf.general*, as in other text-based sites in cyberspace, what people "say" *is* what people "do"! The interesting task in analyzing the posts in this space is in making a distinction between what participants say participants should do (say) and what participants "actually" do (say). A form of *textual* analysis (sociocultural) as opposed to (historical) *document* analysis has been developed in the field of literary criticism but its base in non-interactive print media limits its application to the more overtly social text of cyberspace.[9] In a text-based site in cyberspace, participation *is* data. It is possible to "read" the data, to observe the social space as I did without making an observable appearance. This is not to suggest for a moment that the act of "reading" is objective or non-participatory, however.[10] What I am suggesting is that methods appropriate to research in cyberspace are nascent.

"Climate" studies focusing on informal institutional practices of inclusion and exclusion suggest appropriate analytic tools. The importance of "the institutional atmosphere, environment or climate"[11] in fostering full participation and development of students and faculty members has increasingly been recognized by a number of universities and colleges. I relate the concept of climate to informal opportunities for and limits to participation in public cyberspace. In terms of textual analysis of the eight threads identified above, this is achieved by focusing specifically on the expression of and correspondence between articulated and actualized norms of behaviour and sanctions for violation of these norms and assessing the *quality of dialogue* overall.

As text is social behaviour in *ncf.general*, my focus on inclusive versus exclusive tendencies with regard to participation in cyberspace is well served by concepts relating to behaviour in social settings. Lave and Wenger's sociocultural analysis of communities of practice provides a foundation for textual analysis of the posts to *ncf.general* in terms of the traditional sociological concepts of norms and sanctions[12]. I identify norms and sanctions relating to participation articulated in threads one through three and compare these with the actualization of norms and sanctions in threads four through eight. As Hodder's distinction between stated intention and action above suggests, revealing both the articulated and the actualized norms and sanctions contributes to an assessment of climate in *ncf.general*.

Within the three threads relating to the public nature of *ncf.general*, participants explicitly and implicitly articulate norms of behaviour for participation and associated sanctions. The description and analysis of threads four through eight reveals the ways in which norms of behaviour for participation and associated sanctions are actually imposed. I include an assessment of discursive style as it relates to quality of dialogue in my discussion of all eight threads. My assessment of the climate of *ncf.gen-*

eral is based on the evidence derived from textual analysis of all eight threads.

In summary, to determine the degree to which inclusivity is achieved in *ncf.general*, it is necessary to work with indicators of participation that go beyond the issues of technical access facilitated by NCF and the foregrounded inequities relating to technological competence, literacy and voice. These indicators are:

- norms of behaviour for participation
- sanctions for violation of these norms
- quality of dialogue

While this book is primarily focused on the analysis of qualitative data, there are two indicators of inclusivity that can be analysed quantitatively. These relate to gender and participation and gender and control of topics.

Quantitative Analysis: Breakdown of Participation by Gender

To determine some of the "whos" in terms of who is actually writing this social space and hence its inclusive nature, I begin with a gendered breakdown of participation in *ncf.general*. Of a total of 2,920 messages posted to *ncf.general* during the two month time period relevant to this study, 2300 are posted by individuals presenting[13] themselves as men, 374 by individuals presenting themselves as women, and 246 by persons of ambiguous gender. If I ignore persons of ambiguous gender for a moment, we see that the ratio of male to female postings is approximately 6:1. That is, for every message posted by an individual presenting herself as a woman, six are posted by an individual presenting himself as a man. If I were to divide the number of postings by persons of ambiguous gender equally between men and women (which I think would be generous) the ratio would still be 5:1 in favour of male-presenting postings to *ncf.general*.

In order to explore further the issue of gender and participation, I counted the number of subject headings during the two month period as well as the gender-presented of the user contributing them. New subject headings are introduced to begin a conversation on a new topic, to re-direct an existing conversation, or to state an opinion with regard to an ongoing conversation. Of a total of 751 different subject headings, 545 are contributed by individuals presenting themselves as men, 130 by individuals presenting themselves as women, and 76 by persons of ambiguous gender. This means that the ratio of men to women contributing new subject headings is approximately 4:1. If, as before, I divide contributions by persons of ambiguous gender equally between men and women, the ratio of men to women posting new subject headings is approximately 3.5:1.

While the ratio of men to women in posting new topics is more equal than in contributing posts in general, an examination of the content of the messages with new subject headings reveals a pattern. From one third to one half of the posts with new subject headings contributed by women are information-oriented. That is, they contain announcements (for example, about NCF events, activities, policies, etceteras, or other organizations in the community), requests for information, or information in response to requests by others. While men, too, initiate information-oriented posts, these posts represent a significantly smaller proportion of their total posts and initiation of subject headings, than the proportion for women. This information about the gender of persons participating in *ncf.general* is important for foregrounding a specific analysis of the gender of the community of practice that is actually constructing the meaning of public through active involvement in conversations about the public nature of *ncf.general*.

Three conversations in *ncf.general* during the period of my research feature participants directly addressing what it means for *ncf.general* or cyberspace more broadly to be "public." This internal discourse of the public contains a total of 143 posts. Of these 143 posts, 107 are made by men, 8 by women, and 28 by persons of ambiguous gender. The ratio of male to female posts is approximately 13:1, a far higher ratio in favour of men than that for *ncf.general* as a whole. If I divide the posts by persons of ambiguous gender equally between men and women, the ratio in favour of men decreases to approximately 5:1, a figure more in line with the gendered breakdown of posts to *ncf.general* as a whole.

The actual number of individuals contributing to these threads is 79. Of these individuals, 61 present themselves as men, 8 present themselves as women, and 10 present their gender ambiguously[14]. This is a ratio of approximately 7.6:1 in favour of men. Dividing the persons of ambiguous gender equally between men and women reduces the ratio to approximately 5:1. These threads contain 12 subject headings in total, contributed by 10 individuals, all of whom are male.

Beyond Counting

Not surprisingly, the quantitative data on gender of participation reveals a hefty imbalance in favour of male participation. This can be attributed at least partly to the causes I outlined regarding the masculine culture of computing in the previous chapter. But is there a more complex story of inclusion and exclusion to be found in this space? It is this story that is revealed by studying select conversations in this space in depth.

Fraser provides inspiration for a more complex analysis of participation in *ncf.general*:

> One task for critical theory is to render visible the ways in which societal inequality infects formally inclusive existing public spheres and taints discursive interaction within them.[15]

Once again, the three conversations or threads that directly address issues of the public nature of *ncf.general* are:

1. Frequent Posters
2. NCF.Board
3. Internet Racism

In "frequent posters", participants debate the appropriateness of presenting statistics that summarize the activity of the particular forum's most frequent contributors to *ncf.general*. These discussions raise a range of understandings of what is meant by "public". In "ncf.board", posts concern the control that the NCF Board of directors does exert, and should or should not exert, over *ncf.general*, its climate, and its participants. The issue of control of a public space is key to this discussion. In "internet racism", debate centers on the use of the internet for the propagation of hate material and on the defense of freedom of expression. The nature of participation in public space and the meaning of public space are thus explicitly contested.

I identify explicit or implicit discourses of the public contained within each of these threads and the norms of behaviour for participation and sanctions for violation of these norms associated with these discourses. As the imposition of norms and sanctions is instrumental in establishing boundaries between insiders and outsiders, I suggest some of the implications of both the norms and sanctions themselves, and the processes by which they are constructed. I analyze the threads in terms of discursive style to establish the quality of the dialogue. The identification of norms and sanctions, combined with an assessment of the quality of dialogue, allows me to begin to take the temperature of *ncf.general*.

1. Frequent Posters

On January 9, a participant identifying himself as Kirk W publishes a listing of the number of posts per participant in *ncf.general* for the month of December. While posts to this thread revealed that Kirk W had provided such a summary in the past for *ncf.general*, the December statistics provoke a discussion about the appropriateness of publishing personal posting statistics. This thread, or focused conversation lasts seven days. During that period, a total of 52 posts are made on the topic. Of these, 48 posts are made by individuals presenting themselves as men and 4 by individuals presenting themselves as women. Eighteen individuals contribute to this thread. Of those 18 individuals, 14 are "male" and 4 are "female". In order of frequency of contribution, these individuals are:

Ryan C	10	Paul P	4
Jason V	8	Jamie P	3
Kirk W	7	Richard H	3

The remaining participants contribute one or two posts.

There are 6 subject headings that comprise the "frequent posters" thread. These are:

- frequent posters
- posting of unsolicited statistics
- more stats on frequent posters
- a spam post
- infrequent posters
- look who takes the numbers to heart

These six subject headings are introduced by 4 individuals, all of whom present their gender as male.

Kirk W's post summarizes the posts to *ncf.general* for the previous month by number of posts per participant. Member names and user numbers are included with the statistics. In total, 319 individual users posted to *ncf.general* in December. Of these individuals, 228 presented their gender as male, 59 as female, and 31 ambiguously. Dividing the number of individuals of ambiguous gender evenly, as above, the ratio of posts by gender for the month of December is approximately 3:1 in favour of males.

It is interesting to notice how the ratio widens considerably as the frequency of posts per individual is analyzed by gender. The top ten presenters are all male. The frequency of their posts is as follows:

Jason V	98	Andrew J	25
Bert R	77	Joe A	24
Jamie P	55	Paul P	21
Ernie T	44	Hugh D	18
David D	37	Keith D	17

The top female posters are as follows:

Bess J	14	Debbie J	10
Janice M	13	Louise L	10
Serena W	12		

Of the 26 individuals contributing 10 or more posts, 19 are "men", 5 are "women", and 2 are of ambiguous gender. Of the 65 individuals contributing between 3 and 9 posts, 52 are "men", 7 are "women", and 6 are of ambiguous gender. Of the 49 individuals contributing 2 posts, 34 are "men", 9 are "women", and 6 are of ambiguous gender. Of the 177 individuals contributing 1 post, 102 are "men", 31 are "women", and 14 are of ambiguous gender.

On January 10, a post appears in which Graham F makes known his objections to the posting of such information. He contests the issues of privacy and the public nature of *ncf.general*:

> What's the purpose of this listing? I object to having personal-use statistics collected and used for unintended purposes. How many (or few) times I post an item, login, send/receive mail is nobody's business but my own and the site administrators for required system admin purposes.

In the statistics provided by Kirk W, Graham F is shown as having made 13 posts to *ncf.general* in December. Jasmine D suggests to Graham F, on January 10, that he "lighten up." She suggests that if he is really disturbed by these statistics that he could ask to have his name deleted. She also points out that these statistics refer only to public postings to *ncf.general* and not to personal use of email. She adds:

> Personally, I enjoy it. If nothing more, just to see how verbose Jason is.

A subsequent post on the same day from Jason V indicates that no offence is taken on his part as he replies to Jasmine D:

> Over 3 posts a day :)

Kirk W responds to Graham F, explaining that the purpose of posting this information is:

> For information . . . it gives many people a sense of who the leaders/big thinkers are in the community. The Youth and Feminism SIGS have these statistics as permanent menu items.

One of the issues that comes up for discussion in subsequent posts in this thread is the degree to which volume reflects leadership and "thinking." In the same post, Kirk W points out to Graham F that the information he has summarized has already been made public:

> The information is freely available to anyone who wants it. I just counted how many times your name is in the "From" line.

The "public" nature of *ncf.general* is addressed explicitly in this thread. Graham F's initial objection to the publication of information regarding participation in *ncf.general* is countered by Kirk W's assertion that the information is already "public." Ryan C joins the discussion by equating the "public" nature of activity in *ncf.general* with surveillance of personal activity in off-line "public" areas:

> The number of times I visit a chiropractor, or Aunti Mabel in North York, is also "public" information in the sense that if you watched my public activities closely enough you'd find out these things. It is "public" activity you'd be watching. But if I found out you were doing it, I'd call the cops.

He further states:

> Yes, yes, you have the right to collect all the stats you want and massage them any way you want, but your data points involve the lives of real people.

In response to Graham F's analogy between visiting the chiropractor and his Aunt Mabel, Andrew J comments that it is a "pretty ridiculous analogy" because:

You're not carrying on private business when you post to a newsgroup. Anyone who wants can tell how many times you've posted, just as they could count how many letters to the editor you'd had printed in your local newspaper.

The comparison of *ncf.general* with the letters-to-the-editor section of a newspaper is interesting. While letters to the editor are selected by the paper, *all* posts to *ncf.general* appear. Acceptance of this letters-to-the-editor analogy has two implications. In the first place, there is an implicit acknowledgement of editorial intervention. It is not my sense that the author of the above post intended to support intervention. In the second place, and entirely in keeping with the above author's message, this analogy emphasizes that posts are public utterances and once made belong not to the individual but to the public domain. This understanding of the posting of messages is specific to a self-professed public site in cyberspace. In contrast, for example, the Well, a fee-based "community" physically based in San Francisco, provides blanket copyright for all participants with the promise/announcement that on the Well "you own your own words." No one may use them without the poster's permission. Conceptions of public space have consequences for the way participants structure the space. It is in this "thread" that conceptions relating to the private versus the public nature of participation in *ncf.general* are debated and a dominant view articulated.

Graham F's objections receive a considerable amount of ridicule on the basis of user conceptions of *ncf.general* as public space. Jamie P makes a number of insulting posts in response. On January 12, he says:

Unclench your a**hole and maybe some air will get to your brain buddy. That was a total of how many PUBLIC messages you posted. Anyone who can count could see how many you posted. If the computer could count how many rediculous things you wrote then I could see you getting all out of sorts.

Some users attempt to address the issues of private versus public more seriously. Ryan C, for example, on January 12, insists that all such statistics should be presented anonymously. Also on January 12, Graham F suggests that Kirk W re-read the NCF Board's policy statement on privacy:

especially the bit about NCF doing it's utmost to safeguard user privacy. Kirk W is a quasi-official of NCF, and I don't think his posting of user NAME & number of postings by that user is within the spirit of Privacy intended by the Board.

On January 13, Richard H insists on the public nature of *ncf.general*, saying:

Funny thing people are crying about privacy. The newsreader displays the posters name right down the right side of the screen. I can just do an author search and count how many times it stops at a name. I see news-groups more like letters to the editor, you have made a public statement in a public forum therefore what does privacy have to do with it! If you truly want privacy then you can either not post, or use an anonymous remailer. I like the fact that I can see who made the post so I can choose to ignore the ones that I wish.

!Dan R informed readers, in his January 12 post, that he had:

originally posted "number of hours connected" stats, also purely pub-lic information, but people objected. Now, you have to grant permis-sion for this information about you to be shown, even though it's already public.

Jamie P insults Graham F again in a post dated January 13. After suggesting that Graham F "go soak his head" in response to his sugges-tion that Kirk W "go policy" (that is, type the command to read the NCF's policy statement on privacy), Jamie P says:

You specifically and deliberately put the information out into the pub-lic domain, now you're claiming it was private??? You are clueless . . . that much is obvious . . . .Public information you deliberately make public is not secret . . . duh!

Another issue that is raised concerns who has the right to collect and publish such statistics and in what capacity. In a post dated January 10, James W states:

I have no objection to such stats if published by FreeNet officially, but I do not understand your reasoning in taking it upon yourself to do so.

Kirk W replies on January 11, claiming that the fem sig. and socialist sig[16]. asked him to provide such statistics and that he has received requests for other discussion areas as well. He explains that he has written a special program enabling the quick assembly of such statistics and will continue to publish them as long as he is requested to do so. Ryan C insists that the NCF Board did not ask Kirk W to collect and publish these statistics:

> Kirk is not acting on behalf of NCF; the Board did not ask him to post that information. If you feel your rights are violated and that Kirk will not change his behaviour, address your concerns to the "complaint" mail alias and the Board will decide the issue.

On January 13, Hilton B contradicts Ryan C on this point and asks:

> For pete sakes Ryan - give it a rest.

He insists that:

> members of the Board are aware of his actions and have used his stats in the past.

Furthermore, he points out that they are very useful:

> A couple of times, based on these types of stats, I have read postings from frequent posters and then approached them to ask them to consider volunteering on the NCF. Frequent users are motivated to keep FreeNet alive. These stats make my job easier.

There is not a great deal of discussion with regard to the content of the list. There is the issue of the significance of volume in terms of whether it represents leadership or "importance". There is also the following post by Arleigh R, on January 11, in support of the publication of the list:

> There is an interesting thing about the list in that it demonstrates (in a small way) how much use the NCF is getting. If you don't want to be included in the list, don't post. What could we possibly have to hide in happy "Nettville?"

The most significant post regarding content is made on January 13 by Bess J. It is worth quoting in its entirety:

As the debate continues, I have to wonder how many people in this group read anything more than the number of times they personally posted. I am pretty obsessive about reading everything but I only read the names of the top twenty and my listing. Things I have learned from this list (in the past):

1. Very few women are frequent posters in this group. Last time only 2 women were in the top twenty (and one was me see next point).
2. People are having problems finding stuff on NCF. Nearly all my posts are "look here for what you want" posts. And that made me the 8th most frequent poster. Obviously we need search tools.
3. There is a large gap between the frequent posters and the rest of the group. It is true that a few people are doing the majority of the posting.

I am also interested in the ratio of posters to lurkers. Without Kirk's list it is hard to compare the numbers given by the "showcounts" tool with the number of unique contributors.

The "frequent posters" thread ends with a few posts exchanged between Kirk W and two other participants about the possibility of posting statistics regarding the actual volume of posts per user. The exchange is restricted to technical issues rather than the ethical questions that were raised about Kirk W's original "frequent posters" post.

In the "frequent poster" thread, the public is conceived of as comparable to public physical space (public streets, etceteras); in terms of the public domain comparable to letters to the editor; or comparable to information available as a matter of public record (the number of times an individual visits a chiropractor, for example). These conceptions are invoked to support competing arguments with regard to the appropriateness of the posting of statistics on the frequency of individuals posting to *ncf.general*. The conception of the public as the same as physical space or public domain in the sense of visiting a chiropractor is used to justify a right-to-privacy perspective in opposition to the posting of such information. The conception of the public as a letter to the editor is used to dismiss any grounds for privacy in an a priori public domain.

These competing arguments represent opposite values and related norms of behaviour as appropriate to *ncf.general* as public space. On the one hand, the right to privacy is asserted. On the other hand, privacy is dismissed as a relevant concept in a context of public participation. Appropriate sanctions or mechanisms of control that are introduced are contradictory as well. Viewing *ncf.general* as public space in the sense that certain physical spaces are public, but where individuals have a right to personal privacy, leads several participants to urge that action be taken by the NCF Board to curb Kirk W's behaviour with regard to the posting of frequent poster statistics. Conceiving of posts to *ncf.general* as public documents leads several participants to suggest that participation in the public sphere is voluntary and that individuals who do not wish their names and the number of times they participate to appear in the statistics on frequent posters should simply refrain from actively participating. Although individuals are informed by a Board member who is participating in this discussion that they are free to complain to the NCF Board if they feel that their rights are being violated, the dominant view in this discussion is that no new, unpublished information is presented in Kirk W's posts. It does seem like an obvious point that individuals who post do so publicly, and that any participant could count the number of times other participants have posted because the information is already there.

Not incidentally, the information provided by Kirk W in the "frequent posters" post was quite valuable to me as a researcher; it was illuminating in terms of "who" was dominating the discussion. That the top ten posters for the month of December were all male is significant and consistent with my findings over the two month period.

The quality of dialogue in evidence in this thread is highly polemical and characterized by personal attacks on Graham F for stating an opinion contrary to the dominant view. Graham F is subjected to considerable ridicule and insult by more than one individual, and other participants do not speak out against such insulting behaviour. The participants, through a combination of text and silence, marginalize the perspective of one participant. While some would say that in this case, the better argument prevails, the dominant discourse is both reasoned *and* insulting. Neither the discursive style of assuming that there is a "correct" perspective nor the practice of ridiculing and insulting the "opponent" is challenged or problematized by any of the participants in "frequent posters".

2. NCF.Board

This thread is arguably less coherent than the other threads analyzed in this study. It actually involves at least two separate "conversations" but all posts concern the issue of the NCF Board of Directors and the control they do, should, or should not exert over *ncf.general*, user accounts and the climate and content of *ncf.general*. From December 29 to January 26, 13 posts are made that directly address this issue. Twelve of these posts are made by "men" and 1 is made by a "woman". In total, 8 individuals, 7 "men" and 1 "woman", contribute to this thread.

There are 4 subject headings that make up the "ncf.board" thread. They are:

- A title eludes me
- board members?
- Now that we're cleaning 1st Airborne
- Why?

All four titles are introduced by individuals presenting their gender as male.

The first subject heading, "A Title Eludes Me," concerns Bert R's claim that as a user who is "well connected" to the NCF Board, Stephanie, exercised undue influence in dealing with an instance where he used language she found offensive. Specifically, in a long, rambling, self-indulgent post dated December 29, 1994, Bert R states:

> The bit with Stephanie had been simmering since I got the second "I don't like it" e-mail from her. The exact quote that sticks in my mind, and still bothers me: "Is it really worth losing your account just because you're having a lousy day." Since Stephanie was the only one who objected, and she had sent me a previous e-mail telling me something was against her taste in language (again, something that didn't work without the word "bitch", which I use the same as "asshole" for a man), I perceived this as a threat. After all, Stephanie is apparently well-connected with the board, and I have a long history of being right and disbelieved, or the rules changed to support the popular person who does me wrong. I make no apologies to Stephanie; I still think her a hypocrite, for some of her (apparent) bigotry in quotation choices.

On the same day, Ursula F responds to Bert R's post with some concern:

> I've been freenetting for about a year and a half and have been an Information Provider for about a year and I'd like to make a few com-

ments about the suggestion that IPs such as Stephanie are "well connected" with the board and therefore are able to get people's accounts yanked. There seems to be a pattern to these accusations of undue influence. I've noticed that it's fairly common for someone who has disagreed with an IP to suggest that the IP has censored them by threatening to delete posts or to yank their account. I've said it before (many times indeed): IPs have very little power. IPs have limited access to the Unix shell - this access enables them to create menus and to add information texts. That's it - no extra time (we fight for modem time too), no extra privileges. The only posts IPs can delete are their own. As I've said before (many times): it is actually very difficult to lose your account on NCF - over the last year a handful have been temporarily suspended and I know of only two or three that have actually been permanently yanked. Suspension or elimination of an account is a Board process - it would require the active intervention of the Board and would be discussed at Board meeting (the details would be handled in camera).

Ursula F continues:

> One of the disheartening things about volunteering as an IP is the regularity with which NCFers assume that I.P.s have power they maliciously misuse. I.P.dom doesn't offer any machiavellian pleasures - it's rather more like being a glorified filing clerk.

The next post that relates to this thread occurs on January 9, 1995. Under the subject heading "board members?", Jason V complains about the behaviour of a Board member. He claims that:

> I had a board member tell me to stop posting on a topic he thought was inappropriate for Ott.General a while back. I deeply resent being told what I can or cannot post about on a general non-NCF newsgroup. He claimed a person pointed my post out to him on ott.general.

Jason V goes on about the inconsistency of Board intervention:

> To this person on the board, you know exactly who you are, where were you when pete went after me Where were you when Janice posted anything? What about otto? Why did Mr. XXXXXX single me out? Ott.general is not under control of NCF in any way.

Jason V then explains the content of the post that prompted action by the Board member:

> The post in question was to ott.general, looking for people who would be willing to form a pro-choice group that would photograph and picket the homes of people who picket doctor's homes. It was non-vulgar, non-profane, and could be read aloud to 11 year olds clutching barney dolls.

Jason V states his objection to this interference:

> I realize that this is free, but I don't think I should have to curtail my posts to suit another person's political viewpoint.

He adds that:

> This smacks of political control of NCF.

On January 9, Jack C responds with the point that:

> the activity advocated in the post might contravene the criminal code. And by posting from NCF, you involve the organization in your advocacy. Profanity or vulgarity online may be a matter of taste or opinion, but unless actual threats are made, libelous statements made, or serious complaints received, the board generally keeps to a "hands off" policy.

!Dan R responds to Jason V's post as well with a similar argument:

> The issue comes down to whether or not one thinks NCF (via its Board) is "responsible" for the conduct and postings of its members. Many Board members feel that NCF is responsible for your postings, and therefore they want control over what you say. This is reflected in the User Agreement we signed. From Clause 1:
>
>> Board of the National Capital FreeNet will be the sole arbiter of what constitutes obscene, abusive, or objectionable language.
>
> If you want uncensored access to Usenet, NCF isn't the place to be posting.

The fourth post under this subject heading, all of which occur on January 9, is made by Jason V. Jason V says to !Dan R that he agrees about NCF not being the place to post if you want uncensored access to Usenet, but his concern is because of the topic of the post that he made and because:

> this was a sole member of the Board acting on his own accord. It was not a decision arrived at by the board.

!Dan R responds to this post by saying that the Board often delegates individual members to act on its behalf:

> The subcommittee that deals with "objectionable language" currently has only one person on it, Dean A (mail to "complaint"). If you think you're being treated unfairly by the subcommittee, you'll have to ask the Board as a whole to over-rule its delegate.

Jason V responds to this post, indicating that he has come to understand the reasons for the Board member's actions:

> I think it was done fairly, with good reason, but I think it should have been made a lot clearer as to why he was doing it.

!Dan Rresponds to Bill's post with the suggestion that he mail Dean A a note to this effect. He says Jason V's concerns in this regard sound reasonable. That is the extent of this particular exchange within the thread.

It is not until January 24 that another post is made that contributes to the larger thread of "ncf.Board". Under the subject heading, "Now that we're cleaning 1st Airborne," Ralph V makes the following suggestion:

> ... how about cleaning up *ncf.general*? When and if I wish to see racist, homophobic, sexually deviant or 'bathroom' humour items, I don't tune in to this area [Try rec.humour to post your infantile fart joke, P.L.]
>
> I'm against censorship, but FOR categorization. If I don't want to see live 'exotic' dancers in a restaurant, I won't go to Fanny's etc. If I attend a church service and the sky-pilot exhorts me to 'burn all <insert-racial/religious/?-group>' then I know I'm out of place. Surely some of the drivel published by ... (you know who) can be taken elsewhere.

Paul P responds with a post on the same day. He posts the following sexist joke:

Hey Ralph,

Hear about the two lawyers walking along a beach when a well built blond in a string bikini walked by?

LAWYER 1: Hey, how would you like to screw her?

LAWYER 2: Screw her out of what?

Ralph V responds the following day:

Very good Paul. You looked into the Canonical List of Lawyer Humour, part 1, (posted Jan. 11 to rec.humour), grabbed joke #151 and substituted for the F word. Glad you're with the program.

While this post appears to be somewhat sarcastic in tone, I observe that Ralph focuses on the issue of profanity while failing to acknowledge the sexism.

On January 26, David R introduces the subject heading "WHY?" in response to Ralph's original complaint about the climate of *ncf.general* and says

Thanks for saying it - I've been wondering as well. The slagging and counter slagging so common on this board are making it a rather unwelcoming place.

These posts are two of the very few on *ncf.general* that address issues relating to climate.

The "ncf.board" thread is unique in my data in that issues relating to climate are explicitly discussed, although no explicit definitions of public space are invoked. Rather, posts reflect the advocacy of specific values in the way that this public cyberspace is controlled. The issues addressed relate to the climate of *ncf.general*, censorship by the Board of Directors, the power and influence of members of the Board of Directors, the behaviour of the Board of Directors, and the user agreement of National Capital FreeNet.

On the one hand, several complaints about the climate of *ncf.general* are made. One participant ask that homophobic, racist and obscene content be re-directed to another area where it would be more appropriate. Another participant adds that the conflict-oriented and insult-oriented nature of discussions is off-putting and creates an unwelcoming climate. On the other hand, the Board's hands-off policy with regard to posts with the exception of threats, libel, obscene language, or serious complaints, is deemed appropriate. This control policy implies a belief in the value of allowing as much free expression as possible and the corresponding norm with regard to behaviour, namely, that pretty much anything goes. The sanction or control mechanism implied with regard to the climate complaints is that of censorship, even though one participant argues that he is supporting categorization not censorship.

Of particular significance is the ultimate acceptance by Jason V, with no contestation from other participants, of the appropriateness of censorship of one of his posts to another discussion group by a Board member. While initially challenged by Jason V, when informed of the need to protect NCF as a whole from criminal liability, he accepts the need for such controls. This is one instance in *ncf.general* when the "rights" of the individual to free expression are transcended in favour of the good of the community as a whole. The lack of contestation to control of this kind by the Board indicates that, in contrast to the articulated values relating to freedom of expression, tacit acceptance of some forms of censorship prevails in practice.

3. Internet Racism

This thread relates to concerns about racism (and other forms of hatred) on the internet. The introduction of this topic to *ncf.general* by a representative of the Canadian Human Rights Commission meets with a response that frames the issue in terms of freedom of speech and censorship. The "internet racism" thread begins on December 25, 1994 and is still underway at the end of the research period (February 20, 1995). Seventy-eight posts are made in this thread during this period. Of these 78 posts, 47 are made by "men", 3 by "women", and 28 by persons of ambiguous gender. In total, 53 individuals contribute. Of these 53 participants, 40 are "men", 3 are "women", and 10 are of ambiguous gender. The top participants in order of frequency are as follows:

reptile[17]   8
mtrede[18]   6

Kelly D[19].   6
Brian J   3
Mark W   3

The remaining participants contribute one or two posts each. There are only two subject headings in this thread:

- internet racism
- can they muzzle your modem?

Both are introduced by individuals presenting their gender as male.

This thread begins clearly with a post made by Steven S on December 25, 1994. Steven S announces:

> I work for the Canadian Human Rights Commission. I am currently doing research on the use of the Internet for the propagation of hate material. The purpose of the research is to determine what measures could be considered to control the use of the Net for this type of purpose. I would appreciate hearing from anyone who has any views, information or comments on this subject or who know of anywhere on the Internet where this matter is discussed.

The public responses to this request (it is reasonable to assume that Steven S may have received private email in response as well) range from inhospitable to openly hostile. Censorship is decried and the freedom of expression many believe possible on the net is heralded as a value worth defending. A number of tangential topics also arise, such as gun control and the relative superiority of Canada over the United States. But it is the discussion about freedom of speech and censorship on the net that is particularly relevant to this study's focus on the public nature of public cyberspace. These discussions directly relate to the issues of access and participation and hence the degree of inclusivity of public cyberspace. They also provide a basis for identifying norms and sanctions relating to participatory behaviour and climate. My description of this thread is therefore concentrated on posts that relate directly to issues of freedom of speech and censorship in cyberspace.

In response to his request for views and information on the possible regulation of hate propaganda on the net, Steven S receives a number of replies expressing opposition to censorship of any kind. The first response is from Jason V in the early morning hours of December 26th. He refers to an intense flame war between himself and Pete R, not to provide an example of hate material on the internet but to take a stand in opposition to censorship:

> A user on this very board wrote a very distasteful and sexist comment about me two days before christmas, ruining what might have been a good night. I had no choice but to insult him back, and basically the whole thing has degenerated into a whinefest. This user is either a nazi sympathizer or an outright nazi, I'm not sure which . . . As much as I think pete is a walking bowel movement, he has the right to voice his opinion.

The "adult" concept of anti-censorship is addressed with juvenile and pejorative language, and no attempt is made to take the conversation to a level of critical discourse.

Keith D, only minutes behind Jason V in responding, expresses a similar opinion somewhat more tactfully, if sarcastically:

> Please let me know if you do find a way to control the net so I may leave it and find an uncontrolled medium.

Later that morning the chorus grows with Gunther H saying:

> I sincerely hope you never find the means to control. We ordinary people are sensible enough to censure oneself, without any government interference. Get lost, and stay lost.

Less defensively, several participants in the discussion suggest that getting bigotry out in the open is a more effective way of dealing with it than by censoring its expression and that participants on the net have ways of marginalizing the voices of hatred without censoring them. As Prever M remarks on December 26:

> I hope you close up your liberal research and give back the rest of the grant money tomorrow. You cannot control the net without resorting to fascist censorship and when you do this, a new portion of the net will appear. It will be a losing battle and should not be subsidized by public funds. Your views are not my views and probably not anyone else's either. Most people on the net are smart enough to recognize hate material and ignore it if offends or fight back if necessary.

Statements to the effect that participants in a group find ways of censoring participation indicates that some participants are aware of the ability of a group to effect participation in a social space through the enforcement of some standards of acceptability. On January 16, Brian J suggests that self-censorship is the appropriate approach to take:

> How often we forget that if we don't like what we see, don't look at it. Much like the TV and my preschool children, I don't like what they see, the TV gets turned off.

The majority of participants in this thread assume that government officials are going to jump into *their* cyberspaces and censor *their* utterances. A number of participants defend with passion the idea that the internet is, and should be, a site where freedom of speech/expression is possible. On December 26, Claudette D makes the claim that:

> the internet is about the only place left where freedom of expression is possible,

in voicing her opposition to what she interprets to be the Canadian Human Rights Commission's "attempt to censor the Net." Sidney W, on January 3, says the following about the internet:

> It is the last bastion of free speech in a society that is control crazed and more and more rapidly learning to live in fear at the hands of media and government "protectors." . . . .This space is a microcosm of all of humanity. It has its good, evil, kind, wonderful and bizarre components, all of which are handled and understood perfectly well by the inhabitants, much like the physical world. (sound scary?) The reaction of government to any problem is control. Not much of a demonstration of faith in the citizenry. Not much of a reason for the citizenry to have any faith in the government . . . .Anyone who helps with government control of the last true "commons" should turn in his/her skin at the first opportunity, assuming they're not skinned for doing it. ENOUGH with controls! We're controlled to death in this country, and you want to choke off the last vestige of air we have. My only hope is enough people will learn about the net to appreciate it and stop the government and the do-gooders before they can get their crippling influence into it. You won't kill it but I'd rather not have to fight to keep it whole. Let there be no doubt, I will.

Joe A suggests in a January 7 post that the original purpose of the "net" is to "aid in the dissemination of information", something that would be compromised by censorship. A later participant points out that nowhere in the user agreement does the National Capital FreeNet mention freedom of expression. Indeed, as Richard H points out in his January 3 post in response to Sidney W's response to Steven S, individuals who have persistently used offensive language have lost their accounts:

> No where in the user agreement is there any reference to FREE SPEECH. In NCF the user does have an acceptable usage policy, albeit vague! Profanity is not allowed, but nazis are? The board has canceled accounts of people using bad language . . . But the racism seems to continue. The thing about these net nazis is the more they talk the more holes will appear in their dogma. Sooner or later (hopefully) they will lose their audience and move away to somewhere else (alt.politics.white.power et al) maybe the easiest way is just not read ANY POSTINGS from those people. You can configure the news-reader to display the posters name. So if nazi1 makes a posting you can just ignore him. Sounds like burying your head in the sand . . . well not really I know that racism exists, but debating these one minded morons will not change their narrow little minds.

The freedom of speech and expression defended with so much emotion seems to be more mythical than real, at least in the context of *ncf.general*.

On January 6, this topic is re-introduced by Bernie T under the subject heading "Can they muzzle your modem?" In a post cross-posted to a number of discussion groups (can.general, *ncf.general*, can.infohighway, comp.org.eff.talk, alt.censorship, alt.activism, alt.skinheads, alt.society.civil-liberty, alt.revisionism, alt.politics.white-power)[20], Bernie T reposts a "recent Usenet news article" posted by Steven S:

> The use of the Internet by white-supremacists, Holocaust deniers, gay bashers and other elements of the extreme right is matter of concern to human rights agencies.
>
> I work for the Canadian Human Rights Commission. I am currently doing research on the use of the Internet for the propagation of hate material. The purpose of the research is to determine what measures could be considered to control the use of the Net for this type of purpose.

I would appreciate hearing from anyone who has any views, information or comments on this subject or who know of anywhere on the Internet where this matter is discussed.

Bernie T informs *ncf.general* that he contacted Steven S personally
to obtain more information about the purpose of this inquiry. He provides a summary of their conversation in this post. In response to a question regarding the legislative authority that would allow the Human
Rights Commission to control offensive speech, Steven S cites Section
13 of the *Canadian Human Rights Act* which refers to:

> Discriminatory practice for a person, or group of persons acting in
> concert, to communicate telephonically, or cause to be so communi-
> cated, repeatedly in whole or in part by means of the facilities of a
> telecommunication undertaking within the legislative authority of
> Parliament any matter that is likely to expose a person or persons to
> hatred or contempt by reason of the fact that the person or those per-
> sons are identifiable on the basis of prohibited grounds of discrimina-
> tion.

Steven S explains that this section of the Act was inspired by a
white supremacist group's use of a telephone hot-line to deliver hate
messages using an answering machine. Steven S informs Bernie T that
although no formal complaints have been made to the Human Rights
Commission regarding the use of the internet for racist messages, such
activity is occurring. Whether the internet would actually fall under this
section of the *Act* remains to be seen. Steven S tells Bernie T that his in-
quiries are informal at this point and not oriented towards producing a
report.

In a post dated January 10, Wayne O asks Steven S and *ncf.general*
participants to keep in mind that:

> the use of the Internet by the extreme left is just as dangerous.

To which reptile responds, on January 11:

> Dangerous to who? I've read many, many posts by leftists and the only
> 'harm' done to me was when I laughed so hard I got soda up my nose.

Robin C posts on January 6:

Personally, I support the ability of you hate-mongers to the same full use of the Internet as everyone else. The Bill Of Rights guarantees freedom of speech and besides, I'd rather have you guys out in the open (where you can fit in my rifle scope). ;)

This reference to the *Bill of Rights* sparks an amusing tangent about the ignorance many Americans demonstrate about Canada when an American participant, reptile, on January 8, claims that Canada has always been rather tyrannical and that:

The Bill of Rights applies only to the United States of America . . . Mr. G is a Canadian, and that fact alone makes me rethink my long-held belief in open borders.

Reptile is obviously unaware that the Canadian *Bill of Rights* preceded the *Canadian Charter of Rights and Freedoms* and continues to be in effect.

Gary Y replies on January 8 to reptile's post, commenting on the ignorance of his/her remarks and explaining that:

Actually, human rights are nearly impossible in Canada: with six months of night upon us it is nearly impossible to get out of our igloos to go down and protest.

Considerable discussion occurs in this thread about the relative merits of Canada and the United States regarding the levels to which democracy is achieved. In "internet racism", democracy is consistently equated with lack of government intervention and with freedom of speech. Several posters challenge the democratic nature of both the United States and Canada by pointing to incidents such as the internment of Japanese descendants in both countries during World War II.

On January 6, Kent S emphasizes the importance of keeping racism out in the open, saying of *ncf.general* that:

Much of what goes on on this list is not exactly "discussion of racial issues," still it is valuable that there is a place where those who contribute to this list can "talk" to one another. Certainly those who contribute to this list would be unlikely to engage in an extended discussion of issues and questions if this list did not exist - indeed it's hard to imagine them speaking to one another at all in other contexts.

The value of *ncf.general* and other public cyberspaces in providing unique opportunities for discussion among individuals who would otherwise never interact is asserted in this post. I address this supposed benefit in my concluding chapter.

The issue of the similarity or difference between speech and action is discussed in this thread and has implications for climate issues in terms of the impact of textual violence on participation. Jesse C on January 8, insists that there is an important difference between what people say and what people do:

> Writing a letter is not the same as throwing a bomb. Insulting a person is not the same as punching them in the mouth.

But, responds David T on the same day:

> we must also realize that sometimes we use words to perform actions (performative utterances). Statements can be used to make a contract or promise, to defame, to damage someone's reputation.

Jesse C posts shortly afterwards acknowledging that libel and slander are exceptions to his previous statement but do not alter his basic position. This issue is taken up again, on January 13 when mtrede expresses the view that it is better to have racism out in the open rather than keep it hidden away. S/he provides an example:

> Humberside here in TO had a problem with racism a few months back, apparently some racist pushed a minority teacher (and I say minority, because I don't know the teacher's race) down the stairs . . . so what does the brilliant staff at Humberside do? They ban red and white shoelaces, a racist sign (or so they say). Now, point out the racists, no? Why not? Can't see em!

On a humorous note, in response to an earlier post by Stan H in which he asserts that "No form of SPEACH IS DANGEROUS," Sidney W says:

> I agree. Most particularly if they can spell. :{

While several individuals note that the NCF *User Agreement* does not guarantee freedom of expression, no one actually takes a position in favour of censorship. The vast majority of participants in this discussion take a position in opposition to formal censorship of any kind. On January 11, Arliss M asks:

> Who will watch the watchman?

Another issue that receives some attention in the form of a few posts concerns the jurisdiction of the internet since it is international in nature.

A post in response to a racist diatribe (examined later as part of "the Long Live Canada (Elliott D)" thread, under the subject heading "Long Live Canada" refers to the "internet racism" thread. Hugh D, on January 13, asks Elliott D:

> So, how long have you been working for the Human Rights commission, and how much are they paying to post such dumb stuff so that they can justify getting their fingers into Cyberspace to strangle out Free Speech?

Hugh D seems seriously to believe that Elliott D is a government rube, inciting racism for some nefarious purpose. The assumption that the Canadian government is out to control *ncf.general* specifically through Steven S's inquiry is shared by a number of participants, even though it seems unreasonable to assume that activities in public discussion areas such as *ncf.general* are significant enough to warrant government scrutiny let alone to assume that government has the resources to "police" the many such sites on the internet. Participants also appear naive as they conceive of freedom of speech as an individual right to say anything at any time in any public space.

On January 16, Bob G asks that this thread not be cross-posted to alt.activism any longer, and provides helpful information regarding "netiquette":

> This thread is an open-ended political discussion, not a resource for activists . . . If you are unfamiliar with such things as editing headers to avoid cross-posts, I recommend that you read messages in news.announce.newusers. Cross-posting to many newsgroups is generally frowned upon because it leads to numerous followups that aren't relevant to every newsgroup the message was originally posted to.

Participants in *ncf.general* are thus encouraged to behave in a socially responsible manner. This encouragement does not elicit accusations or complaints relating to censorship and indicates, consequentially, that there is some general acceptance among participants of some standards of appropriate behaviour on *ncf.general*.

By January 18, most of the posts relevant to this discussion concern the tangential issue of gun-control, a topic that emerged as a result of discussions about democracy and government control. With reference to gun-control legislation proposed by Justice Minister Allan Rock and in response to mtrede's insistence that we should deal with insult by fighting back "with our own words", Mark W says:

> And just what country do you live in? Here in Canada our "beloved" Mr. Rock tells us we are not allowed to "fight back" when threatened physically so what makes you think we will be allowed to "fight back" verbally either? It is true that falsehoods will fall apart under scrutiny. Hence if someone doesn't want their falsehood to "fall apart" they will not allow the scrutiny. The leadership of this country does not want a citizenship which "fights back" either physically or verbally. They want a citizenship which will "roll over" and submit to whatever they tell us.

Another tangent that takes on life from this point concerns the role and value of Canada's international peace-keeping forces.

The last post in this thread during the period of the research returns to the original discussion about offensive material on the internet and what to do about it. Juliet L, under the subject heading, "Freenet - Freedom of Speech," recommends the following:

> You can do what I do, read the first line, if you don't like then q and go to the next message, don't read any posting under that topic and find one that you do like.

She goes on to say that:

> You cannot shut everybody up, you should know that by now, people are going to express themselves no matter what, you just gave your opinion and I guess others are allowed to voice theirs. Remember these discussions get quite heated and those words would be spoken no matter where these discussion takes place, yes in a restaurant. So like I said if you find it offending quit and go onto something else.

Not one participant in this thread speaks in favour of formalized controls to address racism and other forms of hate material on the internet or in *ncf.general*; no one problematizes issues relating to climate.

In "internet racism", debate centres on the use of the internet for the propagation of hate material and on the defence of freedom of expression. The nature of participation in public space and the meaning of public space are thus explicitly contested. In this thread, definitions of cyberspace as public space in general, and *ncf.general* as public space in particular, are multiple. They are as follows:

- *ncf.general* as a public space is a microcosm of all humanity
- *ncf.general* as a public space is "the last true commons"
- *ncf.general* as a public space is committed to freedom of information
- *ncf.general* as a public space is not governed by a guarantee of freedom of expression
- *ncf.general* as a public space is committed to democratic principles, one of which is freedom of expression, and the extent to which this is achieved determines the extent to which it can be said to be democratic and the extent to which it can be said to be public
- *ncf.general* as a unique public space allows individuals to interact who would not otherwise do so
- *ncf.general* as a public space is comparable to physical public spaces such as restaurants
- cyberspace, whether public or private, is subject to government control and regulation

The last definition is certainly the most marginal in the discussion. It is the view implied by Steven S who is considering the propagation of hate crimes on the internet as relevant to existing human rights legislation. The vast majority of participants endorse, implicitly or explicitly, a definition of the public and a view of cyberspace that is in opposition to formal censorship of any kind. One or two participants note that the weight of majority opinion aside, there is nothing in the NCF user agreement guaranteeing freedom of expression but they do not actually take a position in the debate beyond stating this fact.

Values associated with the majority conception of *ncf.general* or the internet as public and hence incompatible with censorship include:

- freedom of expression
- freedom from government interference or regulation
- open forum for racist beliefs does more good than harm; open expression of racist beliefs exposes the ignorance of the perspective

- all opinions are valid (except those in favour of regulation or control)
- freedom of information
- participants should govern their own public spaces

This is in contrast to the minority discourse (implicit only in the initial post by Steven S and in his relayed email conversation with Bernie T) that considers hate propaganda to be a human rights issue and protection from discrimination, whether in public or private forums, to be the responsibility of the government.

Sanctions or mechanisms of control are posited as appropriate to a public space that is predicated on freedom of expression. These include:

- get hatred out in the open where ignorance can be exposed and contested and as a result racists will lose their audience
- participants in a public sphere impose some standards of acceptability - participants marginalize voices of hatred without censoring them
- participants censor themselves
- participation in public space is voluntary so those offended should avoid reading offensive material; individual control in the form of "participate at own risk"
- ignore racism and other forms of hatred

Implied in the minority perspective of hate propaganda as a human rights issue is that there is some legislative authority over what can be said in cyberspace, just as there is over other forms of media. As previously mentioned, however, it is unlikely that Steven S was interested in *ncf.general* when he inquired about internet racism. Participants rather naively and self-importantly jumped to this conclusion.

It is important to note the policy of NCF in this regard. The NCF Board is legally responsible for content and Board members will censor posts containing obscene language, threats, or content which provokes serious complaints[21]. So even the "last true commons" is subject to some social control.

As mentioned in relation to a request that individuals stop crossposting to other discussion groups, there is evidence of tacit acceptance of some standards of behaviour or "netiquette". That encouragement by other participants or even the NCF Board for adherence to certain standards of behaviour is not protested as censorship is revealing. The majority of participants take strident ideological positions, demonizing censorship and idealizing freedom of expression. In practice, however, encouragement to behave in a socially responsible way or assertion of the right of the NCF Board to delete posts containing offensive language is received without protest. However, the preponderance of ideological positioning on many significant topics prohibits critical dialogue that would allow participants to consider and explore issues relating to climate and participation in *ncf.general*.

Dominant, Marginalized, and Missing Discourses of the Public in *ncf.general*

The implication of dominant discourses of the public found in these discussions is that a social space should be as unregulated as possible, a place where individuals participate at their own risk. The value of individual freedom of expression overtakes community-oriented considerations of climate and offensive content. The only controls that are articulated as appropriate are those administered by participants and these are limited to voluntary behaviours such as ignoring offensive materials and marginalization through debate and competing discourses. Marginal but formally uncontested discourses of the public include NCF's official *User Agreement* that does not guarantee freedom of speech but insists upon adherence to some standards regarding offensive, threatening or libelous language. According to the information provided in *ncf.general*, very few individuals have actually lost their accounts and the significant amount of truly offensive sexist, racist and homophobic content as well as exchanges of personal insults indicates that a user would have to go very far over the line indeed to lose privileges. And, as will be noted in the following chapter, textual violence occurs without resulting in informal or formal sanctions.

The suggestion that conversations of hatred and polemical posts create an unwelcoming and/or discriminatory climate is a marginal discourse of the public in *ncf.general*. . The very possibility of textual violence is dismissed for the most part with the assertion that speech and action, save for libelous or defamatory remarks having the capacity to damage a person's reputation, are very different things. While not intending to diminish the material consequences of physical violence, I contend that the injury done to individuals through textual violence is "real." In particular, such injury has a negative effect on inclusivity and hence the public nature of *ncf.general* by discouraging participation.

Posts to *ncf.general* problematizing such content or participatory behaviour, let alone posts asserting the need for mechanisms for controlling either, are rare and considerably underdeveloped. The dominant discourse emphasizes "freedom to" rather than "freedom from" within the public space and this has the likely effect of limiting participation in informal ways.

Such notions of public space entail definitions of access and participation that are little more than nominal, that is, a space is considered "public" as long as an individual is technically able to access and participate in this space. Beyond the two posts in "ncf.board" making the point that the proliferation of offensive language and polemical style has an unwelcoming effect, there is no discussion in *ncf.general* as to the ways in which the climate of a social space, as reflected in norms and sanctions relating to behaviour and quality of dialogue, encourages the participation of some individuals while discouraging the participation of others. Indeed, the response to one of the only two posts raising issues relating to climate is to post a sexist joke. The sexist content of this post is not contested.

The "public" is "written" in *ncf.general* by a small number of very "vocal" "male" participants who emphasize "freedom of expression" while flaming expressions of the public contrary to theirs. The norm of "anything goes," accompanied by an articulated sanction to the effect that "if you don't like it, leave," is more accurately interpreted in practice as "anything goes as long as we agree with it". If "we" don't agree with it, the sanction applied is a barrage of hostile posts to the offending participant. In practice, such a sanction seems bound to ensure that the offending person will "not like it" and hence "leave" or at least retreat to silence on the contested subject, thus becoming an "outsider". The way in which Steven S's question regarding discussions of censorship of the Internet resulted in numerous hostile posts, repeatedly identified him as unwelcome, indeed, as an "outsider." The belief in the overriding value of freedom of expression is justified with the assertion that exposing something to scrutiny (which in practice amounts to flaming) exposes its falseness. This is the public that is written and this is how it is written.

It is worthwhile to summarize how the *rules* of the dominant discourse, that is, the dominant norms and sanctions relating to behaviour, play a part in shaping the climate of *ncf.general*.

As noted above, participants in threads relating to the nature of the public sphere are overwhelmingly "male". This means that "women", explicitly or implicitly excluded from traditional conceptions of the public sphere and many actual public spaces, have in this context "failed" to contribute equally to the social construction of this space. Almost nowhere in the discussions do individuals challenge the dominant discourse of "participate at own risk" with personal testimony about the negative effects of hatespeak. In "internet racism", Jason V does discuss the homophobia directed at him by Pete R but he attaches it to support for freedom of expression. In "ncf.board", two individuals point to the unwelcoming and/or annoying climate resulting from offensive language and polemical debate. But there is no problematization of the exclusion that results for individuals, women, gays and lesbians, people of colour, who find themselves the targets of such hatred. These voices are missing and given the vociferousness of the posts regarding freedom of speech and the value of keeping the internet an uncontrolled medium, it is likely that these discourses would be hotly flamed. The polemical nature of *ncf.general* makes it unlikely that persons wanting a more inclusive public cyberspace will speak up.

In the three threads described and analyzed above, individuals who voice unpopular opinions receive poor treatment. It is reasonable to expect that such an example deters the participation of others. The literature on classroom climate is consistent with this expectation.[22] Flaming as both behavioural norm and sanction seems to be dominant in this sphere. Flaming can be expected to both limit and prevent participation, and therefore diminish broad participation in *ncf.general*.

When broad participation is prevented some individuals are intimidated out of participating and certain conversations and conversational styles are foreclosed. Given the way in which individuals are marginalized along with their opinions for going against "the grain," it is impossible to know what voices, what participatory styles, what perspectives and what topics are being excluded from *ncf.general*. The conversation is controlled by a dominant group who combine a large volume of posts with a traditional style of argumentation characterized by polemics and insult. Majority discourses are articulated that likely limit participation and hence the possibility for a more temperate and inclusive climate. The ways in which controversial topics concerning traditional bases for exclusion are constructed is analyzed in the following chapter to emphasize this point.

My research and the way I have reported it reflects an interpretation of the "public" nature of *ncf.general* as well. I have treated the posts as public declarations, that is, statements by individuals in a public arena. This interpretation supports my reporting of these conversations, much as I would conduct and report an analysis of contents of other media such as television, newspapers, radio. Nevertheless as my purpose is to explore the inclusive nature of *ncf.general* rather than to reveal the individual behaviours of contributors, I have changed all names/userids.

NOTES

[1] Sheila C. Alder, "National Capital Freenet," in *Sea Change*, Volume 5, June 5, 1998.

[2] Somewhat ironically, however, Freenet charges affiliates a fee to use the name. In 1994 the fee was raised to a heft $2000 per year, an amount that forced some affiliates who were struggling to survive (Vancouver Freenet, now the Vancouver Community Net, for example) to break away .

[3] *By-Laws of the National Capital FreeNet Incorporated*, (go bylaws), NCF, 1994.

[4] Ann Game, *Undoing the Social*. (Toronto and Buffalo: University of Toronto Press, 1991), p. 5.

[5] Lynn Cherny and Elizabeth Reba Weise, eds. *Wired Women: Gender and New Realities in Cyberspace*. (Seattle: Seal Press, 1996).

[6] Ian Hodder, "The Interpretation of Documents and Material Culture" in *Handbook of Qualitative Research*. Norman K. Denzin and Yvonna S. Lincoln, eds. (Thousand Oaks, California: Sage Publications, 1994).

[7] John Van Maanen, *Tales of the Field: On Writing Ethnography*. (Chicago and London: University of Chicago Press, 1988).

[8] Ian Hodder, "The Interpretation of Documents and Material Culture" *in Handbook of Qualitative Research*. Norman K. Denzin and Yvonna S. Lincoln, eds. (Thousand Oaks, California: Sage Publications, 1994), p. 395.

[9] For example, see Daniel Cottom, *Text and Culture: The Politics of Interpretation*. (Minneapolis: University of Minnesota Press, 1989).

[10] Patti Lather, *Getting Smart: Feminist Research and Pedagogy With/In the Postmodern*. (New York and London: Routledge, 1991).

[11] Roberta M. Hall and Bernice R. Sandler, *The Classroom Climate: A Chilly One for Women?* (Washington, D.C.: Project on the Status and Education of Women, Association of American Colleges: 1982).

[12] Anthony Giddens, ed. *Introductory Sociology*. (Houndmills, England: Macmillan Press Ltd., 1981).

[13] It is impossible to determine the gender/sexual identity claimed/assigned by individuals posting in this site. It is also, likely, irrelevant to identifying issues relating to participation as research to date indicates that gender-presentation reinforces cultural norms regarding male and female identity and entitlement to so-

cial space. As mentioned in Chapter One, regardless of the "Real Life" gender identity of participants, research indicates that gender norms tend to remain static in cyberspace discussions.

[14] I make no assumptions about whether this ambiguity is intentional or not. In a number of instances, I identify as ambiguous names that could apply to both sexes. In such instances, unless the content of an individual's posts specifically includes an identification of gender, I categorize the participant as having an ambiguous gender.

[15] Nancy Fraser, "Rethinking the Public Sphere: A contribution to the Critique of Actually Existing Democracy, in *The Phantom Public Sphere*, Bruce Robbins, ed. (Minneapolis: University of Minnesota Press, 1993), p. 13.

[16] Specific discussion groups at the National Capital FreeNet where the focus is on feminism and socialism respectively.

[17] This is a name similar to the participant's official username in terms of what I consider to represent ambiguous gender.

[18] This is a name similar to the participant's official username in terms of what I consider to represent ambiguous gender.

[19] Names such as "Robin, Kelly, Chris" make gender assignment difficult. Unless gender is unambiguously presented in posts by the participant, I designate such names as ambiguous in terms of gender, as I do in this case.

[20] "Cross-posting" refers to the practice, much frowned upon by seasoned net users, whereby an individual posts exactly the same message to a number of discussion groups. This practice accomplishes the proliferation of opinion and information with little possibility of engaging with other participants in all the groups.

[21] "go policy"

[22] Roberta M. Hall and Bernice R. Sandler, *The Classroom Climate: A Chilly One for Women?* (Washington, D.C.: Project on the Status and Education of Women, Association of American Colleges: 1982).

CHAPTER 3

Policing the Subject— Social Control in *ncf.general*

The description and analysis of specific conversations relating to traditional bases of exclusion from the public sphere in *ncf.general* form the basis of this chapter. These threads exemplify conversations relating to gender, race and sexual orientation. They provide an opportunity to explore the extent to which the norms and sanctions identified in the previous chapter are operationalized. I identify actual practices relating to inclusive, versus exclusive tendencies and hence the public nature of *ncf.general*. I then complete an assessment of the climate of *ncf.general* as exemplified by the articulation and actualization of these norms and sanctions and the quality of dialogue. Of particular importance is an examination of the ways in which these norms and sanctions construct and reinforce the boundaries between insiders and outsiders in this virtual "community."

These five threads are:

4. Violence Against Women - (Janice M)
5. Reform MP for Nanaimo-Cowichan
6. Racial Purity/White Supremacy (Ernie T)
7. Long Live Canada (Elliott D)
8. Bert R's Signoff

The assessment of climate, in terms of the quality of dialogue, that began to emerge in the previous chapter is developed further in analysis of discussions that directly relate to categories of difference historically employed to justify discrimination and exclusion.

4. Violence Against Women (Janice M)

This thread concerns, in some respects, the topic of violence against women. I have included "Janice M" in the title because ultimately, the thread is oriented as much around her personality and behaviour in *ncf.general* (and other areas of NCF) as it is around the more general issue of violence against women. Indeed, that the thread becomes constructed in this way contributes to an understanding of the ways in which norms and sanctions are used to limit participation in *ncf.general*.

The "Violence Against Women (Janice M)" thread is already underway when the period of my study begins. December 21, 1994 features a number of posts relating to posts made by Janice M. From December 21, 1994 to January 29, 1995, there are a total of 100 posts that can be considered part of the "Violence Against Women (Janice M)" thread. Of these 100 posts, 85 are made by individuals presenting themselves as men, 11 by individuals presenting themselves as women, and 4 by persons of ambiguous gender. These posts are contributed by 35 individuals - 27 presenting their gender as male, 6 presenting their gender as female, and 2 presenting their gender ambiguously. The top posters to this thread are listed below in order of frequency:

Bert R	17	Janice M	4
Jason V	10	Retro	3
Jamie P	9	Christopher W.	3
Donald T.	8	Gordon C.	3

The additional 27 individuals posting to this thread contribute either one or two posts each.

There are 16 subject headings in the "Violence Against Women (Janice M)" thread. In addition, there are five subject headings that relate to the thread incidentally, that is, they include references to Janice M that have little or no direct bearing on the discussion the post is part of. The 16 subject headings that relate directly to the "Violence Against Women (Janice M)" thread are as follows in order of chronological appearance:

- Seasons Greetings
- NO! Simply means NO!
- Women being raped and murdered?
- Listen and Learn

- For Janice M fans
- Janice M - Spam Artiste Extraordinaire
- Attitude
- A Humble Suggestion
- Read this Clayton S
- My new year resolution
- Janice M "needs a sex change"
- Crazy Poster Award
- The Grow Up and Stop Acting Like an Immature Jerk Award
- I think I Got It . . . it . . . put . . .
- Thank God for Janice M
- sig files

Joining the thread in progress makes it impossible to state originator of subject heading with certainty, but careful consideration of the content of conversations under the subject headings "Seasons Greetings" and "NO! Simply Means NO!," leads me to believe that Janice M initiated them. While not as reliable as for the subject headings that were introduced during the period of my study, my analysis of the numerical breakdown of the initiators of primary subject headings is presented below.

Of the sixteen primary subject headings, 10 are initiated by "men", 4 by "women", and 2 by persons of ambiguous gender. In total, 10 individuals initiate all 16 primary subject headings. Of these ten individuals, 7 are "men", 2 are "women", and 1 is an individual of ambiguous gender. The initiators of subject headings are listed below in order of frequency:

Janice M	3	Retro	2
Bert R	2	Donald T.	2
David D	2		

The additional five initiators contribute one subject-heading each.

In addition, there are posts made under other subject headings that contain incidental references to Janice M. These will be discussed following an account of the posts that make up the primary thread.

A number of issues form the bases of discussions in the "Violence Against Women (Janice M)" thread, not the least of which is the personality/sanity of Janice M herself. While the basic "topic" of this thread is violence against women, as much, if not more attention is devoted to Janice's personality, her sanity, and how participants in *ncf.general* should deal with her.

The first post during the period of this study that relates to the "Violence Against Women (Janice M)" thread occurs on December 21, 1994 under the subject heading "Seasons Greetings." In this post, David D prefaces his response with a quote from an earlier post by Janice M. This Janice M post may have kicked off the discussion under the "Season's Greetings" subject heading. Janice M's words, quoted in David D's post are:

> You know who you are, I won't tell your names, but guys I want to tell you that I hate you from the bottom of my heart and I wish you a terrible new year. Don't call me a man hater, because you are not men.

David D's responds to this post saying that he regrets the above "poisonous" message defiling the "holiday spirit" and says that he prays:

> that the gods will bring you a good man who will make you happy and who will show you what love is like.

The second post in this thread appears under the subject heading "NO! Simply Means NO!" In earlier posts, as indicated by the pieces of text Bert R splices in between his own remarks in this post, Janice M has addressed the subject of sexual violence against women and asserted that "No means No". Bert R challenges Janice M regarding generalizations about male violence and inserts pieces of his own and her previous posts with additions by him to present what appears to be a dialogue, or a bivocal argument that is nasty on both sides. In particular, their "argument" relates to who is crazy and in need of counselling. One issue that Janice M has raised concerns Bert R's signoff file (a thread in itself which will be analyzed subsequently). Bert R's signoff file is:

> There is nothing so beautiful as a woman at the peak of ecstasy. And nothing so satisfying as bringing her there, repeatedly.

Janice M accuses Bert R of sexism in this signoff and he disagrees with her.

In a subsequent post, Bert R refers to Janice's "rants" on the Fem.sig.[1] Ultimately, under the subject headings "For Janice M' fans" and "Listen to this Clayton S" he posts samples of her posts to other NCF discussion groups on *ncf.general*. Bert R does this in order to dissuade two male participants, Clayton S and Gordon C, from supporting Janice

M - not only with respect to her assertion that "No means No" but with regard to her objection to his signoff.

Under the subject heading "women being raped and murdered?", Ernie T, a self-avowed white supremacist, questions an earlier statement by Janice M that violence against women is epidemic, that "women are being raped and murdered with impunity." There is discussion about the meaning of impunity among participants. On December 21, 1994 Suzanne M responds to Ernie T's questioning of impunity with a short post:

> December 6, 1989, Ecole Polytechnique in Montreal, Marc Lepine, does THAT ring a bell?[2]

This post is met with challenges from a number of men regarding the degree of impunity with which Lepine committed this act. Janice M responds to dismissals of her assertion that women are being raped and murdered with impunity with a December 22 post:

> Men are not women, they cannot understand how women feel. We are always in fear. We cannot go to the corner store without looking over our shoulders. We get assaulted on the streets. We get assaulted at home. Men view us as sex objects. This is what I call impunity. Has any man been jailed for accosting a woman on the street? No because men control the justice system and they root for their co-abusers. Don't tell me that we are not abused with impunity because you have never and will never know fear.

Janice M provokes considerable outrage from a number of male posters as a result of her statements in a brief exchange of posts on December 21, 1994 with Jason V. With regard to her Seasons Greetings post "guys I want to tell you that I hate you from the bottom of my heart", Jason V tells Janice M "I'm not a man. I'm intersexed" and asks if she hates him anyway. Janice M responds:

> Does it mean you have a penis? If you do, lose it. Then we can become friends. As long as you have a penis you are my enemy, it is a deadly weapon used to hurt women.

Jason V responds with humour at his own expense that his penis, such as it is, is so undeveloped that it hardly constitutes a weapon:

I suppose in close quarters I could take an eye out or something, i've never considered using it as an assault weapon. If one put a tiny helmet on the front and tried using it as a battering ram, perhaps it would be useful in combat.

While Jason V's description of himself as "intersexed" sparks a flame war between a self-professed neo-nazi homophobe named Pete R that takes up considerable space on *ncf.general* for the following week, it is Janice M's assertion that the penis is a weapon and that to be her friend Jason V must "lose it" that sparks a number of hostile posts from outraged male participants.

A number of participants remind Janice M that she would not exist if not for the biological role played by the penis in reproduction. One such post is contributed, on December 22, by Craig B:

> to use Janice's logic, her dad should have cut his dick off before using this deadly weapon on her mom. Ergo, no Janice. Hey, I'll drink to that.

Also on December 22, Jamie P says:

> Guess what Janice half of everything you are came out of a penis! A penis can be used to please a women, or to hurt a woman, it depends on the man.

Jamie P subsequently makes a rather threatening post to Janice M that trivializes the violence she has experienced (another participant makes reference in another post to Janice M's reported experience of having being raped in her home by a man who transmitted the HIV virus to her):

> Hey Janice! Santa is a man Janice! Santa has a penis. He likes to have little kids on his lap. He's going to break in through the chimney Janice. You can't get away he knows if you've been bad or good. He knows when you are sleeping, he knows when you're awake. He's made a list . . . and you're on it, he checks it twice. Hey isn't that a reindeer up on the roof now? Merry X-mas Janice grin

In spite of an earlier comment by an NCF Board member, cited in the previous chapter, to the effect that the Board will censor threatening posts, the textual violence in this post is perhaps too "subtle" for official action. Or perhaps only material that elicits formal complaints is acted upon. This post remained available two weeks after it was originally made. Since only the author of a post or a member of the NCF Board acting in an official capacity could delete it, the reason for its absence would not be crystal clear. But its continued presence makes it clear that it does not receive official attention or it is not deemed offensive enough for removal. In any event, the textual violence in this post goes unchallenged, officially and unofficially, as no participants problematize the implicit threat contained within it.

Effort is made on the part of several posters to keep the focus on the issue of violence against women and in particular the issue of consent to sexual relations. Katherine W relates her experience of attempted sexual assault where a drunken male friend attempted to sexually assault her one night. She relates how he called the next day to accuse her of being a cock-teaser:

> he was drunkenly wrong the night of the incident, and soberly wrong
> the next day when he called.

While suggesting that the influence of alcohol is a factor in creating confusion around the issue of consent, Katherine W insists that male perceptions regarding issues of consent are problematic in themselves.

In response to Katherine W's post, a number of male participants in the discussion blame women for "playing games", for saying "no" when they mean "yes". There are several challenges from a number of men to Janice M's generalizations about men as perpetrators and women as victims. Several male participants attempt to address the issue of consent and violence against women seriously. In a post under the subject heading "Listen and Learn," Janice M quotes messages of support and agreement from several men with regard to her comments about violence against women and consent. She suggests that the men who are arguing with her on *ncf.general* can learn from the posts of the men she quotes. Both Gordon C and Clayton S make posts in support of Janice M's assertion that "No means No". Bert R, as mentioned earlier, responds to Clayton S's post with a warning that he had better watch who he is allying with and by compiling samples of Janice M's posts to other discussion groups. In this way, he deflects attention away from the issues relating to violence against women that she (and other participants) are raising by focusing on Janice M's personality. This is highly consistent with the tra-

ditional, attack-oriented discursive style described in Chapter Two and is
one example of the ways in which attempts to raise the discussion on
ncf.general to a more critical level are thwarted.

On December 23, a male participant points to the problematic influence of media by pointing out that:

> On the one hand we cry out that violence against woman has to stop
> and yet on the other we actively promote its continuance through what
> passes for entertainment on TV.

Bert R believes himself to be contributing to the discussion of this
issue by relating an incident when, in a state of inebriation, he attempted
to sexually assault a female friend. While he decided to forgo drinking
heavily in the future as a result, and while he reports that she understood
and forgave him, he ends his post by emphasizing that women often tease
men to the "danger point."

Janice M's posts and the heated responses to them provoke considerable discussion about her personality, how to handle her, etceteras.
Shane S accuses Janice M, on December 22, of having an "attitude problem". While he acknowledges that the problems she raises are not new,
he says that most women "don't whine every chance they get." In response to Janice M's admonition to men to listen to women when they
say no, to have their brains rather than their penises control their behaviour, Bert R says:

> Janice, learn to stop having your rapist's penis control your brain.
> You're a very sick person.

Subsequently, Bert R informs participants in *ncf.general* that in the
past Janice M has sent death threats to David D via email. On December
22, David D explains his decision not to make complaints about Janice
M's threats either to the NCF board or to the police by insisting that it
would be a waste of time. He subsequently encourages participants to ignore Janice M under the subject heading "A Humble Suggestion," on December 23:

> It seems to me that Janice thrives in attracting attention. Maybe if we
> ignore her she might change her attitude and start to listen.

The day before, on December 22, Jim C, under the subject heading
"Janice M - Spam Artiste Extraordinaire" suggests, in commenting on

the intense flame war that Janice M's comments have sparked, that Janice M might simply be "spamming." Steve B responds, on December 24, that a spam is a post that is completely irrelevant to a discussion group and that Janice's posts are effective at provoking flame wars and hence fall into another category altogether, presumably that of "flamebait." Jason V subsequently adds a concurring definition of "spamming."

Numerous posts contain insults to Janice M and questions with regard to her sanity. One subject heading that constitutes an insult in itself is introduced by an individual of ambiguous gender. Retro introduces the subject heading "Janice M needs a sex change" on December 27. S/he says

> May be this chick who is filled with so much hate needs a penis or a dick what ever you want to call it . . . she should get a sex change and become a man . . . probably that's what she was in her previous life.

In spite of his earlier "humble suggestion" that the best way for participants to deal with Janice M is to ignore her, David D responds in a post on the same day that:

> What Janice needs is a brain transplant.

Bert R's claim that Janice M alienated the participants in the fem.sig is echoed by Jasmine D.

Although the insults and jokes at Janice M's expense are numerous and encounter little objection during the height of this thread - between December 21st and December 28th - things change once the thread has petered out. A change occurs in "community tolerance" with regard to continued Janice-baiting. For example, on January 12, Allan R, obviously reading the still available posts from the peak time period of the "Violence Against Women (Janice M)" thread, responds under the subject heading "NO! simply means NO!" by saying:

> "I thought it meant "Harder, faster!"

Trevor W responds, only nine minutes later, under the same subject heading, with the statement:

> This (is) fully-inspected, government-approved Grade A flame bait. Have a nice day.

There is only one other response to Allan's post. Scott B, on January 12, replies to Allan R stating that he does not believe that this comment is constructive or worth posting and that he sees no benefit in reviving the discussion. Even more illustrative of the "mood" of *ncf.general* with regard to further insults to Janice M is the response Donald T receives when he introduces the subject heading "Crazy Poster Award" on January 8, 1995, with the recommendation that it be awarded to Janice M. Bess J responds to Craig's suggestion, on January 9, by introducing the subject heading "The Grow Up and Stop Acting Like an Immature Jerk Award". She criticizes Donald T for behaving like a "clueless newbie"[3] and says that

> For someone who has complained to the FreeNet Board about Janice's posts, you sure seem to delight in deliberately trying to create an even more antagonistical situation.

Adam J echoes Bess J's statements and her subject heading on January 10 with the observation that the electronic medium has the potential to create a permanent impression of someone's personality from a passing mood:

> Funny thing about electronic asynchronous communication, you get in a weird mood, make a bad post or two and you have to live it and get roasted and toasted hourly as if it was "you." I like to think she just had a bad day or week or whatever. It happens to the best of us. The electronic world moves quickly and you can get caught up in things before you know where they've taken you . . . .We all have bad days and make bad posts. I like to think we can all forgive and appreciate where each other are coming from and maybe even one day laugh.

Not satisfied with Adam J's "live and let live sentiments," Bess J responds to him on January 10 by saying that:

> We could also be incredibly sick of Donald T's non-stop baiting of Janice M.

Donald T's "non-stop baiting of Janice M" is evidenced when, starting on January 22, 1995, in posts on topics completely unrelated to the "Violence Against Women (Janice M)" thread, such as "Why do we need a military?" and "Airborne Disbandment," he uses a quote by Janice M as his signoff:

I do hate men, I hate them because of their violence and their callous-
ness. If more macho men like you die, it will mean more peace in this
world.

Janice's words, part of one post that she made on only one occasion,
are thus repeated over and over, every time Donald T posts, on any topic.
The response he receives for this action is far from favourable. Jason V
accuses Donald T of being violent by attacking Janice M without provo-
cation, in the form of using her words in his sig.file. An argument ensues
between Jason V and Donald T as Donald T responds with a new subject
heading "Thank God for Janice M" and justifies his use of her words in
his sig.file with the assertion that this society is full of professional victims and that Janice M's words reveal, contrary to her own statements,
that violence is not a male characteristic only and that her words should
be remembered for a long time.

Jamie P, introducing the subject heading "sig files," asks Donald T:

Couldn't you have picked a quote from someone a little more reasonable for your .sig file?

Shane S also challenges Donald T, agreeing with Jason V that Janice
M "has been flamed enough." This exchange, I would argue, represents
an "enough is enough" norm and corresponding sanction of reprimands,
with regard to the continued harassment and baiting of Janice M. In actu-
ality, then, the norm of "anything goes", identified as the articulated
dominant discourse in the preceding chapter, is subject to limits. The
range of limits to the articulated norm of "anything goes" that are actualized in these five threads is discussed later in this chapter.

Janice M is referenced in discussions beyond the 16 primary subject
headings. Donald T's sig.file is an obvious example, but her name is
mentioned, throughout the period under investigation for this dissertation. For example, in a discussion of racial purity/white supremacy, when
Ernie T is accused of compromising his beliefs to "get a chick into bed"
his January 1, 1995 response is the comment:

BTW, I said "love". I didn't say "getting a chick in(to) bed". Maybe
Janice M is on to something after all.

Donald T's "Crazy Poster Award" is another example of how, on
ncf.general, her name lives on in spite of the fact that, after December 27,
she ceased to post to this area. It is my contention that Janice M becomes

a referent on *ncf.general* for both feminism and crazy women. This is an effective means of avoiding taking the issues raised in this discussion seriously.[4]

While Janice M's behaviour in this thread is hardly conducive to creating an inclusive public space, the treatment she receives reveals the way in which sanctions are used to isolate her, to restrict the possibilities for discussion of issues of concern to women more generally, and to impose a hegemonic construction of masculinity. By focusing on Janice M's personality as aberrant, participants effectively make an "outsider" of her and by association, marginalize feminist topics and women's voices. The sanctions that are actualized to achieve this marginalization are insult, ridicule, and textual violence. It is not until such insults are totally spurious (when the thread has been dormant for several weeks) that a norm of "enough is enough" is articulated and imposed. The textual violence contained in Jamie P's threatening post is never problematized. The dominant norm of "anything goes" with the implicit qualifier "as long as we agree with it" contained in the threads discussed in Chapter Two is actualized in the "Violence Against Women (Janice M)" thread.

In addition to marginalizing feminist topics and women's voices, the most vocal participants in this thread impose a hegemonic or orthodox construction of masculinity by attacking men who model less aggressive and less misogynist masculinities. As Connell emphasizes,

> most men benefit from the subordination of women, and hegemonic masculinity is the cultural expression of this ascendancy.[5]

Connell goes on to observe that

> Hegemonic masculinity is constructed in relation to women and to subordinated masculinities. These other masculinities need not be as clearly defined - indeed, achieving hegemony may consist precisely in preventing alternatives gaining cultural definition and recognition as alternatives, confining them to ghettos, to privacy, to unconsciousness.[6]

By attacking male-presenting participants for "allying" with Janice M and dismissing the efforts of these men to take feminist concerns about violence against women seriously, the dominant participants in this thread establish as hegemonic a masculinity characterized by sexism, competitiveness and aggression through textual violence.

In the "Violence Against Women (Janice M)" thread, abusing Janice M takes on the characteristics of a fiercely competitive "sport"[7] with the dominant male-presenting participants attempting to out-do each other at Janice M's expense. Men who problematize such behaviour and hence this orthodox construction of masculinity are marginalized along with Janice M, at least while this thread is at its height. Participation by women and by men associated with subordinated masculinities is hence effectively discouraged.

5. Reform MP for Nanaimo-Cowichan

A number of threads make sexual orientation a more or less constantly debated topic in *ncf.general*. These include "Rosanne Skokes"; "Homosexuals very sick"; and the "flame war" between Jason V and Pete R arising out of his self-identification (in the "Violence Against Women (Janice M)" thread) as being "intersexed" or "between" genders. I have selected "Reform MP for Nanaimo-Cowichan" for textual analysis because it is a thread that relates to legal rights for gays and lesbians and the costs of this identity in the public sphere. It is also reasonably discrete as a specific discussion that emerges, evolves, and then clearly shifts away into little more than an argument organized around a homophobic rant, a shift that is typical of the treatment of sexual orientation as a topic in *ncf.general*.

This thread begins on January 3, 1995 and winds up, more or less, on January 13, 1995. Over this ten day period, 93 posts constitute an intense discussion about the statements of Bob Ringma, the then Member of Parliament and member of the Canadian Reform Party for Nanaimo-Cowichan, a constituency on Canada's Vancouver Island. Sixty-nine of these posts are contributed by "men", 13 by "women", and 10 by persons of ambiguous gender. In total, 31 individuals contribute these 93 posts. Of these individuals, 25 are "men", 2 are "women", and 4 are persons of ambiguous gender. The following is a list of contributors in order of frequency of post:

Serena W	12	ROBIN	4
Jonathan L	9	Martin H	4
Andrew J	7	Pluto	4
Bert R	7	Kevin D	3
Jason V	6	Reginald V	3
Charlie N	5	Mike K	3
Craig S	5		

Each of the remaining participants contribute one or two posts.

As is apparent from the list of subject headings below, the introduction and modification of subject headings is integral to the content of this discussion/debate. The nine subject headings that are part of this thread are, in order of chronological appearance:

- Nanaimo's Homophobic Reform MP
- Oh boy, another flamebait post
- Nanaimo Politically Incorrect Reform MP
- Maritime Flambe
- For Paul
- Should be "Hooray for Skoke"
- To Gay or Not to Gay
- Judging by actions?
- Sexual Orientation? Lesbians? Gays? Very Sick!!

Four of these subject headings are introduced by "men", one by a "woman", and four by persons of ambiguous gender. In total, 7 individuals introduce new subject headings - four "men", one "woman", and 2 persons of ambiguous gender.

On January 3, 1995, Kelly T, a reporter for the *Nanaimo Times*, in her/his only contribution to this thread, sparks intense discussion by posting an article s/he had published in that paper in *ncf.general* under the subject heading "Nanaimo's Homophobic Reform MP". The article, entitled "Brotherly Love? Not in my riding," says Nanaimo MP" is a report/opinion piece about the statements of Bob Ringma, Member of Parliament for Nanaimo-Cowichan with regard to lesbians and gays. Ringma is quoted as saying that homosexuality is "repugnant" and that he supports amending the *Canadian Charter of Rights* to permit discrimination against homosexuals. Ringma is further quoted as stating that he is unaware of any lesbians and gays in his riding that he may be failing to represent. Ringma's reputation for racism regarding the Vietnamese and First Nations' communities within his riding is also noted. Kelly T argues that a public figure is required to represent *all* of the people within his or her riding and that Ringma, with his publicly racist and homophobic statements, is failing in his public duties.

The issues that emerge as the bases for discussion in this thread include the standards of conduct for public officials, the debate about protection against hate crimes versus "special rights" for minorities, the right to privacy versus the right to inclusion, homosexual behaviour and activity itself (specifically anal sex), the relative invisibility of lesbians, the percentage of homosexuals within the population, the origins of homosexuality, the number of gay politicians, the homophobia common to all political parties, legislation regarding employment practices, assumptions regarding sexual identity, the legal definition of sexual orientation, acceptable versus unacceptable homosexual practices and behaviour, and notions of democracy and discrimination. Of particular significance in this thread is the open participation of one out lesbian, who in fact is the most frequent poster in this thread, and two openly gay men.

Serena W's arguments against homophobia and discrimination are augmented by the following quote from Charlotte Bunch included in her signoff.file:

> Our very strength as lesbians lies in the fact that we are outside of patriarchy; our existence challenges its life.

As the highest single contributor to this discussion, Serena W posts 12 times. This lesbian-positive quotation therefore appears 12 times. In other instances, Jonathan L and Martin H self-identify as gay men and insist that homophobic participants in this discussion see the people who are the object of their insults and hatred.

Early responses to Kelly T's post focused largely on the responsibilities of persons in public office and the nature of democracy. Andrew J, for example, in a post dated January 3, contests Kelly T's assertion that the right to express personal views as a private citizen is different from the right of expression of an elected public official who must represent all of her/his constituents whether s/he agrees with them privately or not. Andrew J insists that democracy means that people can hold differing viewpoints and that this applies to public officials as well as to private citizens. Andrew J challenges Kelly T's statements regarding Ringma's racism and homophobia. The issue of the special obligations of public officials is taken up subsequently by a number of participants in the debate.

Jason V responds to Kelly T's post by introducing a new subject heading that demonstrates his awareness of the volatile nature of discussions relating to sexual orientation: "Oh boy, another flamebait post." He agrees with Kelly T regarding the distinction between privately held views and the obligations of public office. Jason V also takes up the issue of the possible percentage of Ringma's constituents who are likely to be lesbian and gay. This issue, too, receives considerable attention in subsequent posts. Steve W, on January 4, asserts that there is a disproportionate number of gay politicians:

> I firmly believe that the numbers of gay politicians is higher than their
> representation in society *because* society has opened up a willing-
> ness to vote for them causing a rush of candidates.

Jason V challenges this assertion by providing an example of a
transsexual politician who was elected in the Atlantic provinces only to
have her office firebombed. She subsequently quit in fear for her safety.
Bert R enshrines (and trivializes) this example in a new subject heading,
on January 5: "Maritime Flambe."

The discussion develops and branches off into polemical and hostile
debates about homosexual behaviour, percentage of homosexuals in the
population, the definition of sexual orientation, and the inclusion of lesbians and gays in anti-discrimination legislation. Anti-homophobic participants in this thread attempt with considerable difficulty and
increasing frustration, to combat the argument that gays and lesbians are
seeking "special rights." For example, ROBIN, on January 7, says:

> Skoke is right on the mark. We need about 295 MPs like her to get this
> country back on the right track. Special laws for special groups (no
> matter which groups) are simply stupid. One law for all is the answer,
> regardless of religion, race, colors, etc., etc.

It is almost possible to "hear" Jonathan L's frustration when he responds to the above remark by ROBIN (spliced into his own post) on
January 7:

> C-41 IS THAT LAW!!!![8]

A considerable amount of "space" becomes devoted to debating the
legal definitions of sexual orientation and sexual preference. There are
those among the homophobic participants in this thread who argue in
favour of including pedophilia and bestiality, but mostly pedophilia, in
the definition of sexual orientation. This causes considerable concern
and heated debate from those who fear the ideological and legal consequences for lesbians and gays. Participants in this latter group argue that
sexual orientation or sexual preference relates solely to gender of preference; not to other aspects of sexual taste. The implication of this debate
concerns legislation protecting individuals from discrimination on the
basis of sexual orientation or preference.

Other intense exchanges occur on the list of issues identified above.
In a post dated January 8, speaking about the ideological basis for associ-

ating homosexuality with child abuse in public debate, Serena W points out that it is easier to blame "others" (whether they be persons of colour or queers) for threats to children rather than acknowledge how close to home the dangers really are. Although this is an important contribution to the debate regarding the definition of sexual orientation, this post receives no response. The attempt by one individual to shift the quality of dialogue to a more genuinely critical level fails. Serena W makes similar attempts throughout this thread with little support from other participants.

At the opposite end of the spectrum with respect to quality of dialogue, one poster is peculiarly focused on gay anal sex - an obsession remarked upon by a number of participants in the discussion. Apparently, Dustin P is well known by *ncf.general* participants for turning any discussion to this topic, regardless of its relevance. Dustin launches himself into the "Reform MP for Nanaimo-Cowichan" thread with definitions of homosexuality and homosexual activity.

Dustin P's first post to this discussion was not available, for whatever reason, when I logged in to *ncf.general*. My awareness of it resulted from a reference to it in a post by Charlie N in which he asks Dustin P what "felching" and "gerbling" are so that he can make up his own mind about such activities. Dustin responds, on January 6 with the following definitions:

> Gerbling: The act of putting live animals (gerbels or other) up the bum. Apparently, they whack on the prostrate producing some kind of pleasure.
>
> Fisting: The act of putting a fist up the bum. This is required of those who have been bumholing for too long, and are now too lose to get any pleasure from bumholing.
>
> Felching: After bumholing. The act of sucking semen out of the bum and swallowing, drooling, or passing it into the recipients mouth.

In case there is any doubt about his opinion of these acts, Dustin P's message also includes that statement that:

> Homosexuality isn't about love. It's about being turned on by more and more elicit behaviour, culminating in the disgusting. It's about how the smell of feces produces an erection. It's just plain grosse.

In commenting upon Dustin P's references to the supposed gay male sexual practices of gerbling, fisting and felching, Craig S suggests about Dustin P that:

he really meant "filching", as in "stealing" - because gay men take his breath away!

Participants who take up this particular topic within this thread from here on challenge Dustin P. Some ask how it is that he knows about all this stuff, and why he is fascinated if he is so grossed out. Others respond by identifying themselves as gay men and distancing themselves from the behaviours Dustin P demonizes. Others point out that sexual behaviour is not specific to gender; that heterosexual anal sex is as common as homosexual anal sex.

A poignant post in response to Dustin P's remarks is made by Martin H. In a post dated January 9, Martin H says:

> I say I am homosexual. You say this means I commit unspeakable acts, acts that should be discouraged and censored from our society without any thought to the context in which they are commited. Maybe I do. Maybe I don't. All I know is that the most sublime part of living a human life has always been to find another to share it with.
>
> You, Dustin, have said many things in your many posts that have made me feel angry and hated. Think carefully. Remember before you say such horrible things, that we all have to live in this society together. Homosexuality has always existed. It always will exist. Deal with it. Live with it.

Serena W makes a similar post on January 6. First of all, she asks why the discussion of the sexual behaviour of homosexuals keeps recurring on *ncf.general*, given the repeatedly available information regarding the risks of a range of sexual practices, hetero- and homo-sexual alike. And on a more personal note she states that:

> Homosexuality is as much about love as heterosexuality is. When I meet a woman and fall in love with her it is every bit as strong as a heterosexual. And making love is just one expression of how we feel about each other.

This draws a comment from Craig S on January 6 about the invisibility of lesbians in mainstream debates about homosexuality. Craig S responds to a post made by Serena W, saying:

> I don't want to minimize your own experience of homophobia, but I would like to mention that it seems to me that the Skokians have a cer-

tain tendency to harp on what gay men do, and completely forget that lesbians even exist. They can't even be non-sexist in their closedmindedness.

These statements and exchanges between members of a minority group are unique in *ncf.general* during the period of my research. While participating in a highly polemical exchange, these individuals model a more critical discursive style aimed at exploring issues more fully and creating a sense of community, at least among themselves as a minority group.

Another central issue that emerges is the relationship between the right to privacy and the right to inclusion. For example, Charlie N, on January 4, makes the following (he thinks) supportive statement of gay rights:

> I think gays have many rights (all that I have) but to insist on the right to approve of terms describing their lifestyle is not one. Some people find liver repugnant, others love it. The problem of two guys Butt Fucking (sorry, it's a fact) is never going to meet with words of praise from most people. It will be tolerated but it can't help but be made fun of or critisized. Hell, gays make fun and joke about straight people.

The issue of the right to privacy or inclusion, queer identity notwithstanding, while discussed above with regard to sexual practices, is actually more significantly situated in this thread within a discussion of employment practices.

ROBIN responds, on January 4, to Kelly T's original post as follows:

> What Ringma did say was that he would support a charter change[9], if necessary, to ensure that employers could refuse to hire homosexuals if they felt it would disrupt the work place.

The very next post disputes such a position. Reginald V problematizes such a provision by suggesting that, for the sake of argument, we replace sexuality with race. Reginald V suggests that such a switch would make obvious how truly discriminatory any such provision would be. Serena W echoes Reginald V's point and in particular the relevance of the historical comparison of sexuality with race when she says, on January 5, that:

Almost 50 years ago it was argued that African-Americans would undermine the effectiveness of the American military, yet desegregation went ahead anyway. It is not the group in question that undermines or compromises a military or a place of employment but rather those negative, often bigoted, attitudes that prevail.

Charlie N argues that there is no need for protection from discrimination on the basis of sexuality because:

being gay doesn't come out in an interview unless there are stereotypical signs that you are.

He then goes on to say, in the case of stereotypical signs of "gayness," however, that:

I have to be honest, that if I were hiring and a screaming queen came into the room I would have a problem hiring him and I would be worried about a lawsuit.

Still on January 5, Serena W responds to this last comment by Charlie N that:

by using effeminacy or aggressiveness as grounds for determining homosexuality you are committing a grievous error . . . The only sure way to know that someone is gay is for them to tell you.

On January 6, Jonathan L responds to Charlie N's "problem" regarding hiring a "screaming queen" by pointing out that not hiring him should he be the best applicant is discrimination. He then goes on to insult Charlie:

you are bigoted. You are a stupid person. Simple as that.

This polemical and personally insulting discursive style is far more typical of posts to this thread, and to "hot" topics on *ncf.general* more generally for that matter, than the few posts noted above where persons marginalized on the bases of sexual identity attempted to bring the conversation to a more critical and socially responsible level. On January 6, C. W puts her/his two cents in with the following comment:

> If it also includes a charter change to allow members of a community to beat the fuck out of "employers," if they "feel" that the "employer" is disrupting the community, it would have more of a sense of fairness to it. This would allow the "employer" the same sort of protection they wish to provide for others.

ROBIN, in a post dated January 7, jumps on Serena W's statement regarding not making assumptions about someone's sexuality and only knowing they are gay if they tell you, by saying:

> So, then, what's the problem in Hiring? Keep it to yourself and there won't be any discrimination. The problem is with those who flaunt their orientation and then use it as a weapon to get special treatment not afforded *all* others.

It is ironic that, beginning on January 2, a concurrent conversation during this period takes place under the subject heading "Honeymoon Help". It involves 3 or 4 posts over a two week period in which the male half of an explicitly heterosexual couple announces that he and his fiancee are planning their honeymoon and asks for suggestions as to where they should go. The "flaunting" of heterosexual identity in this and other instances is never problematized.

Serena W responds to ROBIN's objection to queers who flaunt their sexuality in a post, on January 7, with the concern that people will discriminate on the basis of their suspicions. Reginald V gets back in the conversation with a post on the same day insisting that existing legislation requires that employers document their hiring practices and justify their selection of the person as the best applicant. He points out that prohibiting discrimination on the basis of sexual orientation is entirely consistent with legislation already in effect.

While not addressing the issue of sexual orientation with regard to matters of employment, Craig S, on January 7, counters Dustin P's homophobic rants with the question:

> what gives you the right to run around frothing at the mouth about what other people supposedly do in the privacy of their own bedrooms?

Jason V finally problematizes the issue of privacy in his January 7 point by stating:

I don't flaunt my sexuality, when you stop dating women in public then
you can lecture others about it. I cannot keep it to myself, any more
than I can keep my skin colour to myself.

Jamie P responds to this issue on January 10 by stating that he would
have no problem hiring a homosexual but:

On the other hand if a flaming queen swooshed in with a fake lisp I'd
give him 2 minutes to get off the property before I had the cops throw
him off. Homosexuals don't bother me, flaming queens need a punch
in the head. You tell me that I wouldn't get in dutch for "descriminat-
ing" against him for being homosexual, when really I'm just repulsed
by a big put on stereotypical effeminate act. You can't tell if someone is
gay but you can spot a queen a mile away.

The insistence that effeminate gay men are deserving of physical violence qualifies as a discourse of hatred and belies the notion, articulated
in the threads under examination in Chapter Two, that speech is not action. Such speech justifies and encourages gay bashing and cannot be
considered apart from the physical violence regularly experienced by
gay men in western society. Nobody addresses these issues in this thread.
   Throughout the "Reform MP for Nanaimo-Cowichan" thread there
are a number of gay jokes. One example, posted by Ken G on January 6:

One Greek soldier wanted to emigrate to North America, but he didn't
want to leave his brothers behind.

Ken G includes this joke under the subject heading "For Paul" who
is known on *ncf.general* for telling jokes, often at the expense of some
marginalized group or other. In a subsequent post, on January 6, Paul
replies to Ken G with a gay joke of his own. Later, on January 7, Paul announces that because of the private emails he has received complaining
about his sexual orientation jokes, he will never tell another. At which
point, he tells another. That complaints about the behaviour of an individual are addressed privately indicates that individuals may feel "safer"
about expressing their concerns in private email than in the public space
of *ncf.general*.
   In the midst of the discussion, which dominates *ncf.general* for at
least a week, Liam D makes a post under the subject heading "Gas." On
January 5, Liam says:

> Human methane expulsions. What do you call it at home. No, I'm not
> weird but, I am bored with the current discussions.

Perhaps this can generously be interpreted as his way of problematizing the current climate of *ncf.general*.

By January 13, the "Reform MP for Nanaimo-Cowichan" thread has given way to a discussion of the morality of homosexual behaviour under the subject heading "Lesbians! Gays! Very Sick!!". This constitutes a significant enough departure from the original post by Kelly T that I consider the thread to be as "finished" as any conversation in as fluid an environment as *ncf.general* ever is.

Of all the eight threads analyzed in detail in this dissertation, "Reform MP for Nanaimo-Cowichan" is the only one wherein an individual presenting herself as a woman is the most frequent poster. Serena W is not only a "woman" but is openly lesbian as well. She participates in this thread without becoming embroiled in polemics. She contributes to the thread without attacking other participants and, almost miraculously, she escapes personal attack. The Charlotte Bunch quotation at the end of each of her posts mirrors Serena's participation in *ncf.general*: just as lesbians reveal the limitations of patriarchy by standing outside it, Serena reveals the limitations of traditional dialogue by engaging in more thoughtful discourse. Her contributions are a model of critical dialogue in that she consistently encourages critical exploration of issues and refrains from attacking those with whom she disagrees. Several openly gay men contribute to the thread but only two of them join Serena W in bypassing the polemics of most of the discourse. Together, these three individuals model a more inclusive style of discourse. Nonetheless, the polemical style of the majority of posts to this thread has a limiting effect on more meaningful exploration of topics under discussion. For example, the social construction of difference in relation to sexual orientation is never explored nor are other questions that are far more interesting than whether or not it should be okay to discriminate against gays and lesbians. The discussion in this thread is limited, for the most part, to the polemics of "right" and "wrong."

While there is a great deal of effort put into educating homophobic posters about the "realities" regarding sexual orientation - legal, social, biological, etceteras - there seems to be little movement (on either side of any debate for that matter) among active posters. It may be that the concern among many of those posting is not to convince other active participants to change their discursive positions but to influence the invisible, "lurking" audience.

This thread also provides evidence of the treatment of "outsiders". Dustin P is identified as "irrational" and is undefended by even Skokes' supporters. Unlike other posters who argue for the right of individuals in a democracy to find homosexual behaviour repugnant, Dustin P dwells in detail upon the presumed sexual activities of gay men. The sanctions used to designate Dustin as an "outsider" are ridicule and insult. Still, unlike Janice M's experience, he is not subjected to threats or textual violence. It is reasonable to speculate that Janice M receives harsher treatment because she directs her anger at (heterosexual) men. Dustin P targets gay men, outsiders already, so he is merely treated as a source of amusement.

6. Racial Purity/White Supremacy (Ernie T)

Ernie T is a "regular" on *ncf.general*. Throughout the two month period of my study, he posts on a number of topics. He is a self-avowed white supremacist. He identifies himself, however, as "racially conscious", particularly in response to accusations from other participants in *ncf.general* that he is a racist. While racist views permeate the majority of his posts, I identify a specific thread that has a more or less distinct beginning and ending. This thread concerns his valuation of the racial purity of the white race and the contestation by other participants of both the possibility and desirability of this phenomenon.

There are a total of 65 posts in this thread, beginning on December 27 and ending on December 30, 1994. Of these 65 posts, 59 are contributed by individuals presenting their gender as male and 6 by individuals presenting their gender as female. In total, 15 individuals contribute to this thread. Fourteen are "men"; 1 is a "woman". In order of frequency, the primary contributors are listed as follows:

Ernie T	17	Louise L	6
Jason V	15	Bert R	5
Brian J	7	Richard H	3

The remaining participants contribute one or two posts each.

There are 8 subject headings related to this thread. They are:

- An Answer from Jason V
- White History Test
- Ernie' Gene Pool Purity

- Hermaphrodite
- the nazi party
- NCF taken over by Geraldo
- MIFLIN droppin in
- t.carleton

These 8 subject headings are initiated by four individuals, all of whom present their gender as male.

The issues addressed in the "Racial Purity/White Supremacy (Ernie T)" thread include the possibility and desirability of racial purity, political correctness and anti-racism, the relationship between racism and lack of education, or homophobia and lack of education, the problem of censorship in relation to racism, white culture, homosexuality and the status of women in Ancient Greece, racial consciousness versus racism, Jason V's sanity, Hitler and World War II, the appropriateness of *ncf.general* for this discussion, and the quality of the discussion.

On December 27, Brian J asks Ernie T if he would dump his girlfriend if she were 1/4 or 1/8th Indian. Ernie T's response? "In a second." The next post in this thread, by Bert B, on the same day, attributes Ernie T's racism and his response to the above question to lack of intelligence. A number of participants in this thread make this same point, namely, that racism and homophobia are the result of ignorance and lack of education.

The next post, also contributed on the same day, by Shane S makes the point that racial purity is not only impossible, but unimportant. Shane S says that he expects that:

> I will get a barage of posts and E-mail on this, but it's all the same on the inside. I don't want to hear anything else on this, so do me a favour and don't clutter my mailbox with replies. I am not racist and never will be.

Ernie T maintains that biological purity is possible and desirable and, often enough, does a good job of poking holes in the logic of some of his critics, although he never effectively challenges their claims that racial purity is an impossibility. He is adept at countering the ineffective arguments put before him. On December 28, with regard to dumping his girlfriend if she turned out to be lacking in "white racial purity", Ernie T says that:

If she'll lie about one thing, who's to say what ELSE she'd lie about? Also, I really don't feel comfortable with the thought of leaving a grab-bag of genes to my posterity. In other words, I'd rather that my kids had a pretty good idea of where they came from.

Brian J responds, 6 hours later:

If your girlfriend just found out she had an ancestor who was Indian, would your response be the same? If so, the honesty criterion is a moot point. I'm sure your kids will have a pretty good idea of the lack of depth to their family's gene pool.

Throughout this thread, there are repeated challenges to the possibility of racial purity. On December 30, Bert R enters the discussion, making this contribution:

As a genealogist, history buff, and cynic, I know how much wishful thinking "racial purity" is. No matter how many facts you produce, such people will cling to their beliefs, because like almost everyone, they need somehow to feel superior. The simple fact is, human populations have been so mobile throughout their history that the whole concept of "racial purity" doesn't work. We're just willing to mount anything that will hold still long enough.

Louise L, with a signoff.file advising users to "Call the National Alliance (a Canadian white supremacist group) telephone answering service!" and the number, enters the discussion, chastising Jason V for his lack of tolerance towards racists and homophobes, saying that the tolerance Jason V advocates:

is fine, as long as it's Politically Correct, right Jason?

Louise L and Jason V argue further about this with Jason V preaching education for racists and homophobes and Louise accusing him of being intolerant in that he does not accept racists and homophobes for what they are. Jason V responds to Louise L on December 30, saying:

I've never tried to reform anyone, and I am far from a bleeding heart. You know, louise, some psychologists say hatred expressed to an outward source is an indication of trouble inside. I started off as a racist, then became a homophobe, and now I hate christians and nazis. I know what my problem is, have you figured out why you hate?

Ernie T's responds to Brian J's question about his girlfriend's racial identity by commenting, on December 28, that posing such an abstract dilemma is typical of liberals. He adds that it seems, according to Brian J, the depth of the gene pool is dependent on:

a glorious mish-mash of mixture, the more the better?

Brian J expands on the original insult with the comment that:

Your gene pool lacks depth if all of its members come from the same wading pool.

Ernie T responds, on December 29, with a list of white people that he claims compose his historical gene pool, including Plato, Socrates, Aristotle, Peter the Great, etceteras.

Brian J captures the nature of this discussion in further posts under the subject heading, "Ernie's Gene Pool Purity." On December 29, he challenges the "whiteness" of the range of European peoples. Jason V points out that the Romans were racially mixed. Jason V, Ernie T and Louise L then get into an argument about Hitler and the racial purity of the Aryan race. An issue that emerges from this exchange is the racial purity of Ancient Greece and the prevalence and acceptance of homosexuality within that culture. On December 30, Jason V argues that:

The old greeks were very much into pedophilia . . . .Is this another example of how whites can't control their sexual impulses? Their gods were also very gay positive. Hermaphrodite originally came from greece . . .

A subsequent subject heading, "Hermaphrodite," takes the discussion of Greeks and homosexuality further. In arguments comparing Ernie T's and Louise L's idealized notion of ancient Greece to what he believes to be his own more accurate view, Jason V points out that women were near the bottom of the hierarchy and that Louise L would not have fared so well. On December 30, Louise L disagrees:

The greeks admired women who were 'white-armed and fine-boned.'
They judged a woman according to many standards, such as fertility,
intelligence, grace, beauty, etc . . . So how, pray tell, would I be at the
bottom?

On December 29, David D challenges the notion of white superiority pointing out that:

A white skin is not what it is cracked up to be. With the ozone layer
going to the dogs, the ones who will be incinerated first are those with
whitest skin. The blackest ones will be the survivors, not forever, of
course.

Jamie P responds sarcastically regarding Ernie T's concern with
racial purity:

THE BLOODLINE MUST BE KEPT PURE . . . otherwise you can't
produce a really good banjo playing mutant redneck. It's so much safer
choosing a girl who's background you're sure of if you chose from
your immediate family ;)

In what seems like an effort to change the nature of the debate regarding racial purity, on December 29, Jason V introduces a new subject heading with a corresponding post, "White history test." He claims
that:

Here is a test based on strictly white culture and famous white people.
There has been a lot of "White pride" activists on *ncf.general* as of late,
and I thought I would give my shot at educating them.

Questions provided include "Who wrote "Carmina Burana"?, "Who
was Laura Secord?", etceteras. Louise L responds, on December 29:

Any idiot with access to a European history book could ace all those
questions, if he were actually stupid enough to WANT to answer this
quiz. I could think up a similar test about Zulu kings, the gay rights
movement, famous Jews, etc . . . and make the questions really ob-
scure and trivial. The point is: who cares? I know enough about my an-
cestors history, and the history of my race. Answering stupid little
people's stupid little quizzes is a waste of my time.

And again, at the bottom of her post is the message to call the National Alliance telephone answering service.

On December 30, Jason V introduces the subject heading "the nazi party" in which he condemns the party and announces that he has posted this message to *ncf.general* and alt.politics.white.power as "the two are now almost indistinguishable." Keith D introduces the subject heading "NCF general taken over by Geraldo" and asks "And I gave up TV for this?" Under a concurrent subject heading, "MIFLIN Dropping in," Richard H comments regarding a post made to a topic other than the "Racial Purity/White Supremacy (Ernie T)" thread:

> What a pleasant relief from all the MASTER RACE posts!!!! With Dan Miflin's posts it made *ncf.general* kind of fun! Not like it is now!!! They should change the name of the group to ncf.nazi or ncf.white-only or possible to ncf.we.are.the.master.race the current threads are making me ill.

Responding to Keith D's post re: Geraldo, Richard H says:

> You are WRONG!!!! Geraldo at least changes his topic every night!!! I am also getting tired of all this Master Race bull.

But then Andrew J pipes up:
There's nothing on lately anyway, Keith. Everything is in reruns. But don't worry, in a couple of days you'll get those two new women's channels! I betcha can't wait. :)

Some participants seem to find Ernie's racism offensive and express the opinion that such discussions do not belong on *ncf.general* but the "joke" at the expense of women included in the above post is not addressed by anyone.

On December 30, Ernie T suggests that the discussion be moved to another location, saying:

> Look, why don't we go over to alt.white.power to continue this discussion? Those that want can follow us, and those that don't can ignore us.

The topic of racial purity continues as a sub-topic within the new thread regarding sexuality in ancient Greece. Ernie T's subsequent posts to *ncf.general* during the period my research include a sig.file with the following quote from Hitler: "Eight cripples do not make one gladiator."

Racial purity as a topic of debate is removed from *ncf.general* at this point, only to reappear in a thread I entitle "Long Live Canada (Elliott D)" analyzed below.

This thread is characterized by highly polemical discourse. Ironically, it is the white supremacist who makes more appeals to reasoned argument and his detractors who focus more on insulting him. The success of a white supremacist in occupying this much discursive space should be noted. The norm of freedom of expression in *ncf.general* obviously includes overtly racist pronouncements. The sanction that is articulated in threads discussed in Chapter Two as appropriate for controlling public cyberspace is to allow the ignorance underlying racist and other discriminatory perspectives to be revealed through opportunities for full participation. Whether or not this has the effect of countering racism or encouraging its expression is a troubling question and will be taken up in my concluding chapter. In spite of the articulated norm and sanction with regard to such conversations, after a point several individuals express the point of view that conversations about the superiority of the white race do not belong in this space.

That a lack of tolerance for what several participants refer to as "master race" postings is ultimately expressed in this thread is significant. There is evidence that participants may resist the public space of *ncf.general* being taken up by white supremacist discourse. The result of this expression of lack of tolerance, while perhaps positive in terms of the climate of *ncf.general*, is not unproblematic for public cyberspace as a whole. After all, the issue is resolved when Ernie T. suggests, in response to complaints, that the discussion of racial purity be moved to alt.white.power, another discussion group facilitated by NCF.

Unlike Janice M and Dustin P whose posts inspire their persecution, Ernie T is not dismissed by being constructed through heated ridicule as an "outsider". While he is mocked, his sanity is not questioned and anti-racist participants actually attempt to engage in reasoned debate with him. This has the effect of giving Ernie T some credibility. While ultimately asked to take his topic elsewhere, he participates in other threads in *ncf.general* on more or less equal footing with the other vocal male participants. His white supremacist views do not discredit him generally.

7. Long Live Canada (Elliott D)

With Ernie T's suggestion that the discussion be moved to alt.white.power, the "Racial Purity/White Supremacy (Ernie T)" thread recedes from *ncf.general*. White supremacy and racial purity as focused conversations are absent until Elliott D posts a message on January 13 under the heading, "Long Live Canada". This thread runs from until January 28 and consists of 44 posts. Of these 44 posts, 41 are made by individuals presenting their gender as male, 1 by an individual presenting her gender as female, and 3 by persons of ambiguous gender. In total, 22 individuals contribute to this thread: 18 "men", 1 "woman", and 3 persons of ambiguous gender. Contributors in order of frequency are as follows:

Elliott D	9	Blake C	3
Jason V	5	Bert R	3
Hugh D	5		

The remaining 17 participants contribute one or two posts each. There are 6 subject headings relating to this thread:

- Long Live Canada
- Incorrect use of word Native
- Elliott D
- Elliott Hits the Mark!
- Homosexual
- None

Individuals presenting their gender as male contribute all 6 of these headings. The total number of initiators is 5. In addition to the six headings that directly relate to the "Long Live Canada (Elliott D)" thread, two posts appear under two separate subject headings. These are:

- Extermination of a Nation
- Black History Month

Both of these posts are explicitly anti-racist. While it is impossible to ascertain intentionality in terms of a direct relationship between the "Long Live Canada (Elliott D)" thread and these posts, the fact that they appear in the middle of it bears consideration. They may indicate a form of resistance to the racism and the limited nature of the debate within the

"Long Live Canada (Elliott D)" thread or they may represent a way in
which people of colour are claiming the public space of *ncf.general*.
These possibilities are considered subsequently.

Elliott D asserts that Canada is in decline as a result of racial mixing.
He claims to be a prophet and warns participants in *ncf.general* about the
threat to Canada embodied in the decline of the white race. His original
post sparks considerable debate. The issues raised in this discussion are
racial purity, Elliott D's lack of education (or his stupidity or his insanity),
white supremacy/white pride, colonialism, misogyny directed at black
women, racism versus racial consciousness, anti-Semitism/Jewish con-
spiracy, the meaning of the term "native," and freedom of speech/censor-
ship. In the midst of the flap created by his "Long Live Canada" posts,
Elliott D drops in a post that is indirectly related to other ongoing conversations. Under the subject heading "Homosexuality," he condemns homosexuality as unnatural. His diatribes have multiple targets.

While announcing that he is neither a racist nor a bigot, Elliott D
claims that Canada is in trouble because it is losing its racial purity:

> The only pure race is the white race. Now the country is full of impure
> races it is in danger of losing its identity. To see my point just look at
> any country led by blacks and you will see that it is in a mess . . . On
> the other hand white countries are full of progress and success. The
> only danger white countries face is from the inferior races invading us.
> We need to stop this madness before it is too late. So let's send the
> blacks back to Africa where they came from. The orientals to asia and
> the Indians back to siberia. Then we will have a truly strong Canada.

Jason V responds to this post several hours later, splicing Elliott D's
text within his own post. This results in the visual effect of a point by
point debate between Jason V and Elliott D. Jason V insists that the "indi-
ans" are the only "Canadian" race and challenges a number of Elliott D's
assumptions and statements, including the notion of white racial purity,
the unity of white Canadian identity and Elliott D's generalizations about
countries led by blacks and whites. He closes his post with the assertion:

> You are a racist, not nearly as entertaining as Ernie, but far less intelle-
> gent.

Other participants attack Elliott D for his lack of intelligence. Donald C, on January 13, expresses the hope that intelligent users will ignore
this "pathetic monologue."

Other participants do not invoke the sanction of ignoring offensive posts suggested by Donald C above and articulated as an appropriate sanction in the "public" threads that form the subject matter of Chapter Two. Elliott D's posts and responses to them by other participants continue. Elliott D insists, on January 14, that:

> whites are brainwashed into being ashamed of their race. Blacks despite their stupidity and laziness and inability to learn are encouraged to be proud of their race. Perverts go naked on the streets shouting gay pride.

An early post in this thread relates Elliott D's racial purity position to the ongoing debate around internet racism and censorship. Hugh D, on January 13, asks Elliott D:

> So, how long have you been working for the Human Rights commission, and how much are they paying to post such dumb stuff so that they can justify getting their fingers into Cyberspace to strangle out Free Speech?

It is unclear, at first, whether Hugh D is serious. But in a subsequent post on January 17, it becomes evident that Hugh D is serious as he again remarks on the coincidence of Harvey G's message that the human rights commission is considering investigating racism on the internet. Hugh D says that he expects to see messages attacking women and abortion rights next. He suggests that if this develops, the NCF Board should be asked to look into the accounts of "these people." In the meantime, he expresses the opinion that the best thing to do with people like Elliott D is to ignore them. Hugh D's concern about the Canadian Human Rights Commission censoring *ncf.general* provides Elliott D with another springboard for hatespeak. On January 14 he asserts that:

> The human rights commission is a Jewish organization. They control it, they run it.

On the same day, Bert R describes Elliott D's post as merely a "well-marinated piece of flamebait." Blake C responds to Hugh D on January 17 that:

> This guy could be considered comic relief from the stress of living with all those government types you mention.

With regard to Elliott D's assertion that racial mixing is the result of the behaviour of "white girls," David D, on January 14 asks Elliott D:

> Could you tell me then, why the "white girls" want to sleep with inferior people? Could it be that they were brainwashed into thinking that the "inferior races" are sexually more satisfying?

One of the ways in which Elliott D is insulted during these exchanges is by attributing his lack of intelligence and sanity to having contracted syphilis by sleeping with prostitutes as Elliott D claims to have done. On January 14, David D asks Elliott D:

> Could it be possible that you got syphyllis, which is now affecting your brain?

Gary T responds on the same day with the remark:

> Unfortunately, this would actually require having a brain to begin with.
> So far, the evidence is against him.

Elliott D is ridiculed and his intelligence insulted. This treatment is similar to that received by Dustin P and at least partially similar to that received by Janice M. It is worthwhile to note that Ernie T espoused similar beliefs to Elliott without receiving the same degree of disparaging treatment. Elliott's discursive style is certainly cruder than Ernie's - he does not write as well as Ernie does - and his claim to be a prophet sets him apart from "reasonable" white supremacists such as Ernie.

Another line of discussion that develops within this thread concerns the meaning of the word "native" and the concept of "true Canada." A new subject heading, "Incorrect usage of word Native", is contributed by Bert R on January 14. Under this heading Bert R objects to Jasmine D's restriction of the terms "true Canadian" and "native" to aboriginal peoples only:

> I get sick of hearing fools imply that I'm not native to the only culture
> I've ever known, and that all my ancestors for three generations (and
> some lines more) were born into.

In arguing with Jason V and eventually with other participants who take issue with his assertions, Elliott D makes a number of disturbing remarks. About Jason V's dismissal of white racial purity, Elliott says, on January 14:

> Not all whites are pure but most are. Our race is being tarnished further
> by all the impure races coming here and sleeping with white girls.

The debate about Elliott D's generalizations about black countries and white countries produces some of Elliott's most disturbing comments. In another part of his argument with Jason V in this same post, Elliott says:

> I know the Caribbean. I used to sleep with the girls for a Quarter each.
> That's how cheap blacks are. For a quarter they sell their body.

The responses to both of these remarks are troubling in that they constitute challenges to Elliott D's racism but not to his misogyny. On January 14, Jason V comments on the contradiction between the two statements in the post, pointing out that Elliott D is admitting to doing some racial mixing of his own. He also accuses Elliott D of hypocrisy, as does Jasmine D when she says:

> Funny that a racist such as yourself is willing to "taint" themselves
> with an "inferior" race.

Jason V speculates that the low cost of prostitutes in the Caribbean is perhaps a sign that:

> the blacks know how to control inflation, and a quarter is actually
> worth something?

Elliott D's response to this, on January 17, is:

> Or maybe black p**sy is cheap.

In response to Jason V and Jasmine D's questions as to why he would have sex with black women given his racist beliefs, Elliott D responds:

> I was not tainted. I still have my white skin I only had the satisfaction
> of having black women spread their filthy legs for me for a quarter.

Elliott D remarks upon this further, in a post dated January 17:

> It wasn't like I married them. I f**cked them and threw them away like
> a used napkin. Nothing more nothing less.

Jason V asks, on January 17, why Elliott D would sleep with women
who he describes as "filthy." In a second post on the same day, he responds to Elliott D's comments about throwing women away like a used
napkin:

> Yeah, you probably say the same thing after you suck off some black
> guy in the bushes. You types are all the same.

Not one post mentions anything about the sexism and misogyny of
Elliott D's remarks.
    Ironically, Elliott D himself objects, on January 21, to the way in
which his critics respond to his statements with insults, saying:

> It is so sad that so many white people resort to insult for lack of inabil-
> ity to express themselfs.

He further states,

> I don't insult. The dignity of my race requires that I act with civility.

No one directly challenges his insults to people of colour and in particular to women of colour. It is interesting that he assumes that at least
some of those who are insulting him in response to his statements are
white. The names of people engaging in this debate, while Anglo-Saxon
or French-Canadian in origin, with the exception of Jasmine D[10], in no
way identify participants as "white." Nor do the participants self-identify
in a way that would preclude their being non-white. This provides an example where at least one participant makes assumptions about identity
consistent with hegemonic norms of public space in "disembodied" and
"anonymous" realm of cyberspace.
    It is relevant to discuss two posts that occur during the period of the
"Long Live Canada (Elliott D)" thread that do not engage directly in debate or discussion with Elliott D or his detractors. These two posts may
constitute moments of resistance to the racist statements of Elliott D or to
the limited scope of the debate or they may simply represent ways in

which people of colour are claiming the public space of *ncf.general*. It is impossible to know without making direct contact with the originators, a research method that is beyond the scope of this book.

Both posts occur at the end of the "Long Live Canada" subject heading. One occurs on January 27, and one on January 28. The first post, under the subject heading "Poem: Extermination of a Nation," is a somewhat long (approximately 250 words) poem about the destruction of native peoples, culture, and the land, resulting from colonialism and the resurrection of native peoples and their relationship to the earth. The poem graphically describes the violence of colonialism as this segment indicates:

> when the westerners came
> the white men
> thieves in the night
> taking with one hand
> and holding with the other
> raping, tormenting and killing
> the men and women he should have known
> as his sister and his brother . . .

The poem attributes environmental strain and natural disaster to the lack of balance for which colonialism paved the way. But it ends on a note of both hope and defiance:

> and as there is light
> there is hope
> that there is sight
> hope that those who have not seen
> for so long
> will see
> and return to a balancing way
> for as voices in song
> rise from the center again
> the resurrection of the living way.

Nothing is provided to contextualize the poem. It just appears as one post among many.[11]

The second post is made under the subject heading "Black History Month." In this post, V. M provides information regarding the purpose of

Black History Month, and an extensive list of events. Given the preceding debate around racism/white superiority/black inferiority, this is a significant post. It resonates with pride and creates a space, however briefly, for black culture and celebration on *ncf.general*.

The last post that relates directly to the "Long Live Canada (Elliott D)" thread occurs on January 28. But the topic of racism and white supremacy are taken up in other threads. In particular, racism and anti-racism are central issues in threads concerning the 41st Airborne, and the minority student-only lounge at the University of Guelph in Ontario, Canada.

Elliott D is constructed by other participants in the thread as an "outsider" through othering behaviour in the form of sanctions. The encouragement of the application of sanctions, such as ignorance, and the prevailing use of ridicule in contesting his statements, indicates that he has violated some norm or norms of behaviour on *ncf.general*. This is an indication that in practice, not "everything goes." As articulated in discourses of the public discussed in the previous chapter, participants do find ways of regulating the social space themselves. Elliott D's racism is disturbing to a number of participants and they combine polemic argumentation with insults and ridicule. A particularly troubling feature of the responses to Elliott D's posts is that unlike his racism, his sexism and misogyny go unchallenged.

The amount of space taken up by Elliott D and his detractors in *ncf.general* is considerable for a period of several days. The value of this discussion is questionable, given its overwhelmingly polemic style. Without the presence of more critical dialogue, the value of providing a public platform for racist and misogynist diatribes is questionable. I return to this issue in my concluding chapter.

8. Bert R's Signoff

The final thread to be investigated is Bert R's sig.file or signoff file. Sig.file refers to a programming option that allows users to create a "permanent" (until they change it) file that is automatically attached to every post they make. In some cases, the individual user simply types in her or his name and email address so that it will automatically appear at the end of each post. Others make a political statement. Serena W's sig.file proclaiming lesbian pride through a quote by Charlotte Bunch appears every time she posts a message and is a significant contribution in itself to the thread "Reform MP for Nanaimo-Cowichan". Ernie T's use of a quote by Hitler as his signoff is a powerful statement as well. Donald T's perpetuation of the "Violence Against Women (Janice M)" thread, and particularly, the flaming of Janice M, through the inclusion of a quote by her as his signoff is another example of the sig.file playing a significant discursive role. Contestation of Donald's inclusion of Janice M's words in his sig.file indicates that other participants are aware of the impact of such a textual device. Similarly, Bert R's sig.file is the topic of debate in *ncf.general*.

When I first logged in to *ncf.general*, I found the following statement at the end of each of Bert R's posts:

> There is nothing so beautiful as a woman at the peak of ecstasy. And nothing so satisfying as bringing her there, repeatedly.

As Kirk W's statistics on frequent posters indicate, with a total of 77 posts, Bert R was one of the most frequent posters for the month of December. In the period of my research, I counted 53 times where these words appeared at the end of one of his messages. It is this sig.file that becomes a topic in *ncf.general*.

The first objection to his signoff during the period of my research is made by Janice M. On December 22, she posts an excerpt from an email sent by a man in support of her statements about violence against women. In his email, this man says to her:

> I don't know about you but the above "signoff" gets me a little concerned. This guy obviously doesn't know it, but his signoff illustrates your comment about social conditioning. He probably thinks there's nothing wrong with it . . .

Bert R replies on the same day, stating:

> You found a person who doesn't understand my .sig. I am just so impressed.

At the end of his post, again we read:

> There is nothing so beautiful as a woman at the peak of ecstasy. And nothing so satisfying as bringing her there, repeatedly.

Still on December 22, Clayton S splices the text of a previous argument he and Bert R have had over Bert's .sig file with new comments. It looks something like this (the numbers in brackets on either side of pieces of text indicate the order within which they were posted):

> [1]There is nothing so beautiful as a woman at the peak of ecstasy.[1] [2]This is a fixation. [2] [1]And nothing so satisfying as bringing her there repeatedly.[1] [2]This is a fantasy. Another of your mysoginist desires to control women. This is a rebutal.[2] [3]How do you derive control from a desire to please?[3] [4]By the expression of your thoughts. This is what you want to happen.[4]

This post encapsulating the discussion continues in a similar vein for another 50 words or so. Clayton S ends the post with the assertion that "No means 'No' and that's the truth."

Still on the same day, Bert R addresses a post to Clayton S, asking:

> How the hell do you derive this crap from a stated desire to bring pleasure to a willing partner?

A few sentences later, he says:

> Little man, if I brought my fantasies into real life, I would be exacting cruel revenge on the people who have most offended me during my life. If you cannot see two consenting partners creating something beautiful as anything other than rape, you are a very sick person.

Bert R then goes on to warn Clayton S about allying with Janice M, stating that he sees in Janice M:

> a person easily capable of mass murder of those who disagree with her.

I am not sure how to interpret the following contribution by David D to this thread. He seems to be spoofing when he presents an adapted version of Bert's .sig file as his own. In a post dated December 26, 1994, David D's version is as follows:

> There is nothing so beautiful as two women at the peak of ecstasy. And nothing so satisfying as bringing them up, and keeping them there.

David D continues to use this as his .sig file for a number of posts.

Another response to Bert R 's .sig is included in a January 1 post by Ernie T:

Another assumption is that people who TALK a lot about bringing women to the peak of ecstasy tend not to do it very much (or at all).

Bert R responds by speaking to the autonomic nature of the .sig file:

Actually, it's the ones who brag about their conquests who usually get nothing. Now, the computer actually "talks" about my belief in beauty; I just inputted it the once, and it's repeated the info ever since. And we all know how often computers get laid. Me? I just enjoy making my SO[12] happy.

Many days later, on January 14, Bert R's post displays a new .sig file:

Previous .sig deleted due to mass ignorance in our society.

However, it is not long before the original .sig returns. On January 17 at the bottom of Bert R's posts we find:

There is nothing so beautiful as a woman at the peak of ecstasy. And nothing so satisfying as bringing her there, repeatedly.

His .sig file does change again, twice, during the period of research. The first change occurs as he puts himself forward as a candidate for the NCF Board elections:

Bert R, Candidate for NCF Board. Against the two-hour time limit, and committed to finding better alternatives. Let's stop chasing ideals and deal with reality.

And finally, as the period of research comes to an end, he introduces a new .sig file:

The first step towards wisdom is questioning.

Personally, Bert R's original signoff made me feel very uncomfortable the first time I read it. My discomfort increased exponentially every time I read the signoff, and given the frequency of Bert R's participation, this was often. My growing irritation was quelled somewhat by the sense that this signoff represented something meaningful for the purposes of my research and by the fact that it did not go uncontested. But translating my personal discomfort into a sociologically justifiable statement about the sexist nature of this sig.file and its impact on the climate of *ncf.general* proved challenging.

In attempting to make a connection between my personal discomfort as one woman and my role as a researcher in reporting my findings, I address both the content of the sig.file and the context within which it was presented. In the first place, the repetition of the sexual imagery in relation to women in a public space has been identified by feminists as problematic, particularly with regard to advertising and the media. Such feminist analyses focus on the limited identities available to women in public discourse; women are traditionally portrayed, when portrayed at all in public discourse, in sexual or domestic roles[13]. Consequently, the way in which this sig.file has the effect of presenting women in a sexual capacity repeatedly in this public cyberspace is problematic.

In the second place, the sig.file is contributed by an individual whose overall participation in *ncf.general* during the period of my research is problematic from a feminist perspective. There is evidence of sexism in a number of his posts on a variety of different topics. I relate the most significant example as follows. In a post in the "ncf.board" thread, Bert R attempts to justify his past use of the word "bitch" as an appropriate way to insult a female participant in *ncf.general*. On December 31, Bert R responds to Liam D's question/subject heading "1995, The Year of The . . . " by posting, "Fully-flamed slag-hag" in obvious reference to Janice M. Not only does Bert R attack Janice M personally but his treatment of the issues raised in relation to violence against women in the "Violence Against Women (Janice M)" thread is dismissive and worrisome. While recounting an incident where he drank too much and came close to raping a friend of his who he claims understood and forgave him, Bert R emphasizes that women sometimes tease men to the "danger point." In the "Racial Purity/White Supremacy (Ernie T)" thread, Bert R dismisses the possibility of racial purity by insisting that "humans will mount anything that will stay still long enough." This statement implies that "humans" are "men" and that women are "things" to be "mounted."

As the second highest poster in the month of December, Bert R's impact on the culture of the board is significant. That this impact is understood by a number of participants as negative for women is evidenced by their contestation of his sig.file. In this instance, sexism in *ncf.general* does not go unchallenged. The means by which it is resisted remains within the realm of the traditional polemical style of argumentation, however. The dialogue concerning the sexist nature of the sig.file is largely confined to the "it is too/it is not" form of debate.

Of greater significance in terms of the quality of dialogue as evidenced by discussion in this thread is the fact that sexism specifically and feminist issues in general are restricted to such polemical debate. Explorations of the construction of gender more generally or in the culture of *ncf.general* more specifically do not occur.

POLICING THE SUBJECT

The actualization of norms and sanctions and the primary restriction of discursive style to the polemic as evidenced in the five threads described and analyzed above reveal a number of ways in which the subject is policed. In *ncf.general*, the subject is policed in terms of topic and content; in terms of discursive style. The subject as participant in the conversation is also policed.

There are three participants in these five threads who are identified by other participants as "outsiders". Unlike the way in which Steven S is identified as an "outsider" in terms of being seen as a "threat" or an "enemy", by virtue of his affiliation with the Canadian government, these individuals are dismissed as irrational, as "crazy." Janice M is identified as crazy on the basis of her having issued death threats to at least one of the participants in *ncf.general*. Elliott D's claim to be a messiah and Dustin P's obsessive ravings about homosexual activity are the basis for their being labeled irrational. Although at least one participant in each conversation explicitly accuses each of the three of being mentally unstable, no one challenges these assertions and there are many implicit accusations in this regard. The sanction that is imposed upon these individuals then is that of labeling them as irrational and hence crazy. Accordingly, they are denied credibility and respect. Rationality is thereby used to delineate between insiders and outsiders in *ncf.general*.

The identification of these individuals as "outsiders" is both achieved by, and perceived as justification for, their treatment on *ncf.general*. They are all subjected to ridicule and insult. Janice M, however, receives unique treatment in the form of textual violence in the post by Jamie P cited above. In considering the reasons for this disparate treatment, it is worth noting that the targets of the posts are significantly different: Elliott D goes after people of colour and Jews; Dustin P goes after gay men; Janice M targets men. The participants who are most vocal in "othering" these outsiders are men, the majority of whom identify, at least implicitly, as "straight." Ridiculing and insulting Elliott D and Dustin P is not the effort in perceived self-defense that responses to Janice M seem to be. After all, Janice M is problematizing the violent behaviour of men. While her discursive style is polemical and her arguments characterized by generalizations, she is raising the very real societal problem of male violence against women. Other participants could raise the level of discussion about these issues to a more critical level. Some certainly attempt to but the targeting of Janice M for insult, ridicule and textual violence by other participants undermine these efforts. The racist diatribes of Elliott D or the homophobic ravings of Dustin P do not challenge the status quo in the same way that issues relating to violence against women do. And again, it is worth noting that it is the racism of Elliott's remarks that receive attention. The misogyny evidenced in his remarks about women of colour is literally, unremarkable.

Elliott D's messianic claims and racist statements are contested by many users on *ncf.general*. In arguing with participants who point to the inaccuracy of his claims regarding the association of the "white race" with wealth and the "black race" with poverty, he asserts that white countries that are not wealthy are victims of Jewish conspiracies. He also makes misogynous comments about women of colour which are NEVER contested. His racism and anti-Semitism are challenged but not his sexism and misogyny. Like Janice M and Dustin P, Elliott D is ridiculed and his intelligence insulted, but unlike Janice M, he is not subjected to violent attack.

Dustin P's obsession with anal sex appears to be well known by regular participants in *ncf.general*. There are serious attempts to contest Dustin P's statements. He is also ridiculed and his ignorance commented upon, but he is subjected to neither textual violence nor threats. The designation of Elliott D and Dustin P as irrational makes them the laughing stock of *ncf.general*; they are ridiculed and insulted accordingly. In contrast, Janice M's designation as irrational involves subjecting her personality to intense and hostile scrutiny and targeting her for textual abuse. During the period of my research, the way in which rationality is used to construct boundaries between insiders and outsiders on *ncf.general* varies according to the gender of the subject being constructed as outsider and the subject of this outsider's attacks.

CLIMATE

In *ncf.general*, especially in conversations relating to identity and embodiment, the climate is not chilly - it's hot! Racism, sexism, and homophobia are common on *ncf.general*. Much of it is contested. Much of it is not. Moreover, the way that it is challenged suggests limits. The tone of discussion on contentious issues (and discussions of race, gender and sexuality are *always* contentious) is almost entirely polemical. Critical dialogue is virtually absent from these conversations. With the notable exception of posts by Serena W, Craig S. and Martin H in the "Reform MP for Nanaimo-Cowichan" thread, progressive (that is, anti-sexist, anti-homophobic, anti-racist) discourse is characterized by personal attack in both form and content. The author's subject matter is discredited and the tone is incendiary. The initiation of constructive discussion does occur but if it is on a topic relating to gender, race, or sexuality, it is as likely as hatespeak to become flamebait. Flamebait sparks a heated and polemical discussion with a considerable amount of name calling and insult. Given the toxicity of the climate in discussions on these topics, it seems likely to assume that users who would otherwise participate do not do so in order to avoid being flamed.

There is evidence of limits on the extent to which individuals designated as outsiders are to be harassed on *ncf.general*, however. While the core of the "Violence Against Women (Janice M)" thread fails to reveal those limits, attempts to revive the flamefest by two different (male) individuals are discouraged by several male participants and a female participant. The sentiment at this point in the conversation seems to be "enough is enough." Analysis of one thread in this case study is insufficient for reaching conclusions about "norms" for flaming on *ncf.general* specifically or public cyberspace more generally. But it is my observation that there is more tolerance for flames in the midst of a discussion than for flames that appear out of context. Perhaps one could conclude, in this brief snippet of cyberspace, that one norm of participation is that flaming just for the sake of flaming is too crass. As Bess J. remarks in response to Donald T's effort to revive the flame war against Janice M, "you are acting like a clueless newbie."

The heated character of conversations on *ncf.general* grounded on traditional bases of exclusion from the public sphere reflects the implications of a dominant discourse of the public that privileges "freedom to" over "freedom from". The articulated hostility to any norms of behaviour and corresponding mechanisms of control results in a philosophy of "anything goes" that is ultimately very restrictive. Only those with cast-iron egos and/or strong motivation to debate a point to the "death," that is, until "truth" is once and for all revealed, are likely to participate in such a hostile climate. While no posts are ever immune from a potential flamewar, posts that are particularly high-risk are those relating to controversial topics, such as notions of identity associated with the body and difference. Furthermore, the volume of inflammatory posts that surrounds such topics leaves very little space for thoughtful comments or inquisitive remarks.

The scarcity of critical dialogue in threads relating to bodily difference reveals that, contrary to the optimism of those who associate anonymity with greater opportunities for participation in public space, the "body" remains a highly contested site. The polemical character of discussion means that where identities are concerned, those whose identities are marginalized in society at large are constantly confronted with dialogue whose content and style places their very existence at the centre of a war. While a few brave souls soldier on, whether against racism, sexism or homophobia, it is rare that progressive remarks transcend the traditional style of argumentation to achieve a modicum of thoughtfulness or recognition that multiple viewpoints do exist. Given the articulated emphasis on multiple points of view in the dominant discourse of the public, it is contradictory but not surprising that there is seldom an indication in practice that people are entitled to differing points of view.

The threads examined above exemplify conversations with regard to notions of difference associated with the body on *ncf.general*. Analysis indicates that the "inclusivity" championed in threads relating to the public nature of cyberspace, while ideologically flawed to begin with, really amounts to a restricted form of freedom for a limited group of people. The small group of predominantly male participants uses a polemical style of debate rife with personal attack to identify as "outsider" participants who "go too far." The fact that the most hostile and violent behaviour is directed at the one person who challenges "them" by criticizing males is of particular interest to me. The creation of "outsiders" through the actualization of norms and sanctions - criticism until the "truth" is revealed - is evidence of the way in which the subject, in this case the individual participant, and I would argue other potential participants, is policed.

The polemical climate frames the possibilities for discussion of topics in advance. Individual efforts to transcend this climate and engage in critical dialogue are rarely successful in the threads I have analyzed. For example, while proud lesbian and gay voices play a significant part in the conversation in "Reform MP for Nanaimo-Cowichan", the overwhelming polemical style of discourse limits the extent to which these voices can be more than constructively reactive. The success of the openly lesbian and gay voices in the aforementioned thread, while not insignificant, is limited. Rarely do individuals who employ critical dialogue to take progressive stances on issues relating to inclusion set the agenda for discussion. Never once in the aforementioned thread, for example, is the notion of distinct gender roles and their relation to sexual orientation problematized. The categories of exclusion on the basis of sexual orientation are not contested. And most of the conversation is restricted to a polemical debate between homophobes and gay-positive participants. The lack of opportunity to contest categories of exclusion is one way in which the subject is policed. The lack of opportunity for thoughtful dialogue is yet another way in which the subject is policed. In these ways, the subject as topic and the subject as individual overlap. The very climate of *ncf.general* reflects and reinforces the interconnected policing of the subject as person and the subject as topic. The policing of the subject in these threads contributes powerfully to the writing of the public in *ncf.general*.

The notion of "policing" has negative connotations and this need not be the case. While I am heartened by the contestation of sexism, racism and homophobia in a number of instances, I am considerably troubled by instances where no such contestation occurs. Creating a more temperate climate in public cyberspace requires the policing of exclusive tendencies - in terms of both discursive content *and* style - as well as rigorous monitoring of the ways in which the policing mechanisms themselves may restrict inclusiveness.

Earlier, I identified the ways in which the public in *ncf.general* is written in threads one through three. The public is written by dominant voices who drown out marginal voices. The quality of dialogue that produces the public serves further to ensure that other voices will be absent. This pattern is also reflected in the ways in which the subject is policed in threads four through eight. The subject is policed through the use of sanctions to enforce norms in such a way as to restrict participation to a limited group. The primary norm of this limited group is communication through a harsh discursive style. Extremes of this discursive style are contested but the dominant discursive style is not effectively challenged.

The ways in which the subject is *not* policed are as significant as the enforcement of norms through more overt sanctions. Silence with regard to the effect of quality of dialogue on participation and with regard to instances of racism and misogyny amounts to a failure to police the public space to achieve greater inclusion. As long as the dominant discourses of the public, as articulated and actualized through text in *ncf.general*, are constructed according to notions of individual freedom rather than collective responsibility for the social space, the policing of the subject will have the effect of decreasing rather than increasing the inclusivity of this public cyberspace.

HOPEFUL SIGNS/WHERE DO WE GO FROM HERE?

Although concrete steps have been taken to address issues related to formal access to the National Capital FreeNet, sociocultural inequities relating to literacy, voice, and technological competence for marginalized groups make cyberspace an exclusive realm. That participation is limited in terms of gender at the outset is indicated by the quantitative data reported in Chapter Two. My analysis of posts by gender-presented in *ncf.general* reveals that for every message posted by a "woman", at least six are posted by a "man", and that for every subject heading introduced by a "woman", almost four were introduced by a "man". This indicates that participation in *ncf.general* is significantly male-dominated. This is consistent with existing research on gender and participation in cyberspace.

My analysis of qualitative data reveals more complex issues related to participation in public cyberspace, particularly the claim that anonymity facilitates greater inclusivity and the ways in which the public is actually *written* and *policed* in *ncf.general*. In *ncf.general* the public is written and policed so as to normalize the behaviour of a dominant minority and discourage the participation of those who fall on the deficit side of the key markers of identity specifically explored - gender, race, and sexual orientation. Norms and sanctions, articulated and actualized, create boundaries between insiders and outsiders and establish parameters with regard to the quality of dialogue. That the resulting climate is not facilitative of inclusive/public tendencies has implications for the significance of the body in social theorizing and for feminist contestation of public cyberspace.

Implicit in the claim that anonymity is conducive to democracy is the belief that in cyberspace we can at last "succeed" in leaving the body behind. The underlying assumption is that this lack of embodiment is liberating. Not only is this notion oxymoronic when pursued to its logical conclusion but the extent to which it is liberating when its illusion is "achieved" in any marginal sense, such as in a text-based site in cyberspace, is not equitably distributed. After all, as Pateman emphasizes, lack of embodiment is an illusion that achieves its ideological capital through the masking of the particular embodiment of a dominant group. The "right" kind of body is re-characterized as the lack thereof in the same way that liberal democratic notions of universality simply re-cast the particular experience of a particular group as neutral.[14] That the equitable distribution of even the illusion of disembodiment is neither possible nor desirable clearly follows from this analysis.

As suggested in Chapter One, "Promises, Promises, Promises", without identifying characteristics being obvious, it is likely that anonymity is read according to assumed norms of universality that are not, by definition, based on diversity. I documented one such instance of the assumption of hegemonic norms of racial identity in the "Long Live Canada (Elliott D)" thread. Although the documentation of one instance is far from conclusive, it is at the very least suggestive of this phenomenon. Further research is warranted to determine the extent to which hegemonic norms are applied by participants in the absence of markers of identity.

As mentioned above, "lack of embodiment" is not evenly distributed. Only producers of the dominant discourse claim/are assigned and benefit from this so-called lack of embodiment, whether contrived through a complex matrix of ideology and division of labour or through a text-based site in cyberspace. In *ncf.general*, people marginalized on the intersecting bases of gender, race and sexual orientation, far from experiencing inclusion through "liberation" from embodiment, find their bodies "under attack" as categories of identity are continually subjected to contestation. The scarcity of critical dialogue throughout *ncf.general* but in particular with regard to threads relating to bodily difference is evidence that the body, far from being irrelevant in cyberspace, remains a highly contested site.

As noted, one benefit of *ncf.general* specifically and cyberspace more generally as unregulated public space claimed by a participant in the "Internet Racism" thread is the opportunity for people who would not normally interact to have the opportunity to do so. In some cases, this means that individuals who would normally have little or no audience for their viewpoints find an audience on the net. While access to a different group of people than would normally be possible might be lauded by some members of progressive social movements as positive, the implications of this opportunity being available to "everybody" - including people like Elliott D, for example - makes this so-called benefit more questionable.

The "contributions" to *ncf.general* of participants who espouse discourses of hatred such as Elliott D further problematize the relationship between anonymity and inclusivity. For these participants, it seems that the very "absence"" of the body in terms of non-face-to-face contact may in fact encourage greater hostility rather than greater inclusivity. One of the key strategies in anti-racist education efforts, for example, involves humanizing the "object" of discrimination so that the person espousing racist beliefs is forced to confront them "in the flesh". "Seeing" the object of racism (or sexism or homophobia, for that matter), as a person, as embodied, rather than as a member of an abstract ideological category such as "them" does not eliminate racism on its own but it removes some of the comfort associated with the posture of discrimination. This view suggests that the anonymity of cyberspace, rather than promoting greater inclusivity through lack of embodiment, is more likely to make the hate-mongers feel more comfortable and protected. In short, the anonymity it provides makes public space in cyberspace less inclusive, that is, less "public."

Informal impediments to participation in *ncf.general* are revealed in the discourses of the public. The way in which these norms of behaviour and sanctions are articulated and actualized with respect to "hot" topics is revealed in this chapter. This "policing of the subject" - in terms of topic, discursive style, and individual as subject - reflects an exclusive climate that both shapes and is shaped by the articulation and actualization of oppressive norms and sanctions. I have identified the ways in which norms of behaviour and related sanctions support the restriction of content to competing "truth" claims and a style of dialogue that is polemical and characterized by personal attack. Opportunities for individuals traditionally marginalized in public discourse and in public spheres is limited by the war-like character of discussions relating to these very differences. Thus, the climate of *ncf.general* is unfavourable as far as inclusive tendencies are concerned, particularly with regard to discussions related to the politics of the body. It is my contention that this climate discourages participation by those who are "othered" in these discourses. We will, of course, never know for sure because so few individuals who are targeted for hatred speak up. And those who do speak up are clearly limited by a traditional style of argumentation that privileges polemics rather than discursive exploration.

It would be poor scholarship and cynical politics to ignore promising moments in the eight threads that make up the data for this study. Resistance to an exclusive "public" does occur on *ncf.general*. Strategies that are explicit or implicit include the following:

- ignore hot topics (especially topics related to gender, race, sexuality)
- post on hot topics without engaging with combatants (example of post of poem "Extermination of a Nation" or lengthy details of Black History Month as a way of claiming the space without engaging)
- argue with racists, sexists and homophobes with obviously no hope of changing the minds of those posting but challenging hatespeak for the sake of the lurking audience
- comment on unpleasantness of the exchange, make jokes, try to change the subject, suggest that the discussion be taken elsewhere
- use non-derogatory humour to reduce the intensity of conversation on hot topics

As mentioned in "Policing the Subject", the two posts "Extermination of a Nation" and "Black History Month" occur during a time when the majority of space in *ncf.general* is devoted to an argument between a racist and misogynist and his detractors. The simple act of claiming space for marginalized discourse and marginalized peoples is an act of resistance, whether deliberately constructed or not, in a public space governed by norms and sanctions that make "outsiders" of "others" very quickly. In a subsequent chapter on suggestions for feminist action I will return to emphasize the value of the mere act of claiming "mainstream" public space.

Additionally, while I have been critical of the way in which norms and sanctions are used to police the subject by limiting discursive possibilities and by creating "outsiders," I cannot deny that I am relieved to see that extreme racist and homophobic views result in an individual being identified as an outsider through the social practice of this space. It is regrettable, however, that it is only the extremists who are "othered" in this way, especially since feminist views are othered by the creation of an extreme feminist as the signifier for all feminist discussion.

Conversational space *is* claimed by proponents of a more inclusive public sphere - individuals post messages in response to racist, sexist, and homophobic contributions by other participants and they initiate discussions from a progressive standpoint. Kelly T's post with regard to the homophobic remarks made by Reform MP Ringma are a case in point. The fact that the resulting conversations become polemical and inhospitable almost immediately reflects the limiting climate of *ncf.general*. But the fact that these posts are made at all is not irrelevant. After all, as mentioned above, one of the forms of resistance is to speak out against discourses of hatred for the benefit of the lurking audience. In this way, progressive participants prevent or at least disrupt the articulation of an hegemonic discourse.

Very little space is taken up in *ncf.general* by discussions between like-minded parties. The few efforts by participants to raise the level of discussion to a more critical level are marginally successful at best. The polemical nature of the discourse presents a powerful obstacle to exploration and exchange.

There are a number of instances, however, where participants go beyond a concern with individual rights to take collective responsibility for the public space of *ncf.general*. These include the apparent norm with regard to flaming out of context. This is in evidence in the "Violence Against Women (Janice M)" thread when Donald T is criticized by several participants for flaming Janice M after the conversation has run its course. And, in the "ncf.board" thread, Jason V backs off when informed that a previous post of his was censored to protect National Capital FreeNet from criminal liability. Jason V accepts the fact that the protection of the public space of NCF as a whole may outweigh his individual rights. As no other participants problematize this explanation by a Board member in this thread, I assume that this principle is tacitly accepted in practice, regardless of the vociferousness of posts in *Internet Racism* putting freedom of expression above all other values. And finally, while not removing the racism from NCF as a whole, or even *ncf.general* for that matter given the nature of subsequent conversations, the complaints made by a number of participants with regard to the "Racial Purity/White Supremacy (Ernie T)" thread and the cooperation of Ernie T in the matter, have the effect of removing this particular offensive conversation from *ncf.general*. These instances of participants taking collective responsibility for this public space are hopeful signs.

Hopeful, too, yet somewhat discouraging because their appearance is so exceptional in *ncf.general*, are the posts by Serena W, Martin H and Craig S in the "Reform MP for Nanaimo-Cowichan" thread. These individuals model critical dialogue in both form and content by contesting the homophobia voiced by a number of participants without resorting to name-calling or polemics. Craig S expands the discussion to include a consideration of the ways in which lesbians are made invisible in homophobic discourses and Martin H makes a personal statement to Dustin P about the pain the latter's statements have caused him. In all her posts, Serena W attempts to raise the level of discussion by going beyond issues of "right" and "wrong" and by foregoing personal attacks. While participating in a heated exchange, Serena W remains "cool." The behaviour of these individuals suggests a model of a more inclusive public. The fact that they are so outnumbered restricts their impact on the quality of dialogue in the thread.

In Chapter One I addressed the question of why those concerned with creating greater justice and inclusivity should bother with cyberspace. The following chapters focus on *how* we might bother.

NOTES

¹ Another discussion group at the National Capital FreeNet.

² On December 6, 1989 Marc Lepine entered the University of Montreal's engineering school with a high powered rifle and shot dead 14 women and injured a number of others. Lepine specifically targeted female students, blaming "feminists" for ruining his life.

³ Someone new to cyberspace and hence unfamiliar with "netiquette"

⁴ Incidentally, it is interesting to note that after the period of formal investigation for this study ended, Janice M continued to be invoked as a referent for both feminism and crazy women on a number of occasions over the next several months.

⁵ R.W. Connell, *Gender and Power*. (Stanford, California: Stanford University Press, 1987), p. 185.

⁶ R.W. Connell, *Gender and Power*. (Stanford, California: Stanford University Press, 1987), p. 186.

⁷ Brian Pronger, *The Arena of Masculinity: Sports, Homosexuality, and the Meaning of Sex*. (New York: St. Martin's Press, 1990).

⁸ In 1994 the Canadian government unsuccessfully attempted to guarantee freedom from discrimination to Canada's gays and lesbians. Resistance to the bill's far-reaching implications resulted in substantive amendments.

⁹ S/he is referring to the *Canadian Charter of Rights and Freedoms*.

¹⁰ Her surname suggests that she is of Indian origin.

¹¹ This post is contributed by a person who identifies themselves with a name which may or may not identify an individual or may or may not communi-

cate something significant. I chose to leave out the name rather than clumsily attempt to change it.

[12] "Significant Other"

[13] Dale Spender, *Nattering on the Net: Women, Power and Cyberspace.* (Toronto: Garamond Press, 1995).

[14] Carole Pateman, *The Disorder of Women.* (Cambridge: Polity Press, 1989).

CHAPTER 4

Educational Change
and the Public Sphere

In the first part of the book, I outlined the utopian promises that are part of the marketing strategy associated with the development and introduction of new information technologies. My particular focus is on the new social spaces fostered by these technologies and the promises for expanded democracy and hence a more genuinely public sphere. Promises that technology is both neutral and liberating and that more inclusive public spaces are now possible appear suspect when we review the history of the western public sphere, the masculine culture of technologies, and the embeddedness of technologies within highly stratified relations of power. The case study of *ncf.general* revealed the importance of climate (freedom from) as opposed to the technological facilitation of communication and an emphasis on freedom of expression (freedom to) in creating more inclusive public spaces. At least in this example, the possibility for anonymity provided by new information technologies did not deliver the promised inclusion.

So why not just condemn the technology and dismiss cyberspace proponents as capitalist idealogues or dupes and invest in more traditional forums for social resistance and equity? As noted in Chapter One, anti-technology proponents would have us do just that. But in rejecting the simplicity of both anti-technology approaches and utopian pro-technology promises, I join Penley and Ross in calling for the creation of a generation of technoliterate sceptics – a citizenry capable of engaging critically *with* and *about* technology.

In her well known "Cyborg Manifesto" , Haraway includes a section entitled "The Informatics of Domination" in which she emphasizes the embeddedness of science and new technologies in global relations of power[1].

> Taking responsibility for the social relations of science and technology means refusing an anti-science metaphysics, a demonology of technology, and so means embracing the skillful task of reconstructing the boundaries of daily life, in partial connection with others, in communication with all of our parts.[2]

Haraway argues that neither the celebration nor the demonization of technology will enable us to resist and explore the possibilities of technology meaningfully. She argues that "From one perspective, a cyborg world is about the final imposition of a grid of control on the planet..."

> From another perspective, a cyborg world might be about lived social and bodily realities in which people are not afraid of their joint kinship with animals and machines, not afraid of permanently partial identities and contradictory standpoints. The political struggle is to see from both perspectives at once because each reveals both dominations and possibilities, unimaginable from the other vantage point.[3]

Our society is changing rapidly and this is exhilarating for some, terrifying for others, and incomprehensible for many. We need to be able to respond to the current postindustrial context intelligently, rather than naively or negatively.

As promised, this latter half of the book is aimed at identifying possibilities for contesting exclusive tendencies in public cyberspaces and expanding spaces of inclusion. I argue that one of the locations for developing a generation of technoliterate sceptics is in our educational system. Educational systems in North America and elsewhere are in a panic to keep pace with computing technologies in particular. Most of this panic is driven by labour market agendas and fears, partly resulting from demands of potential employers on the system to provide a computer literate workforce but largely as a result of the social, political and economic consequences of new information technology driven restructuring. The shift to the information age has facilitated a new global economy and produced many economic casualties. There are few indications that this increasingly widespread unemployment is temporary.[4] Current government and school focus on expanding computer competency is a superficial and unsatisfactory response to this restructuring. My call for a greater role for the educational system in negotiating the role of new information technologies in society has a deeper focus.

Rather than merely preparing students to engage *with* the technology and no doubt perpetuating existing social inequality so that the majority will work *for* the technology while an elite minority will *control* it, technoliteracy as an educational focus will combine technical competency with a critical awareness of the embeddedness of technology within social relations. Too few decisions about technology are open for public debate and few of us are competent to penetrate the insider jargon of the technical world. Educational institutions can provide students (and faculty members) with a sense of entitlement to participate in decisions about technology, the knowledge to engage meaningfully, and the skills to contribute to the construction of inclusive dialogue.

Assuming that technology will not be absent from the future of the students we teach, I support Penley and Ross's call for the creation of a technoliterate critical mass. While acknowledging that "the odds are firmly stacked against the efforts of those committed to creating technological countercultures," they argue that there is a "pressing need for more, rather than less, technoliteracy - a crucial requirement not just for purposes of postmodern survival but also for the task of decolonizing, demonopolizing, and democratizing social communication." [5] Technoliteracy is the work of the classroom.

LEARNING TO ENGAGE WITH AND ABOUT
NEW INFORMATION TECHNOLOGIES

Introducing new technologies into our classrooms is an activity of great consequence, because, like other technological change, it is the re-tooling of the social. Postman reminds us that

> New technologies alter the structure of our interests: the things we think *about*. They alter the character of our symbols: the things we think with. And they alter the nature of community: the *arena* in which thoughts develop.[6]

In arguing that technological change is ecological, Postman says that

> It is not possible to contain the effects of a new technology to a limited sphere of human activity . . . one significant change generates total change.[7]

It is not enough for educators to provide students with a map of the information highway. There are critical questions to consider about highways in general, and how humans travel through their environment. By recognizing technologies as social in origin and social in consequence, we provide ourselves with a much needed critical foothold to engage *with* the technology, and to engage *about* the technology.

Research and debate in classrooms at all levels about the politics of technology should surround any skill building technology curriculum.

LEARNING HOW TO WRITE THE PUBLIC

Lave and Wenger[8] bring our attention to the situatedness of the learning process in communities of practice. It follows, therefore, that behaviours of both inclusion and exclusion are learned in community. If public spaces that are more genuinely inclusive are possible, and I refuse to give up this possibility, members of our society need to learn to behave in ways that encourage rather than discourage broad participation. In Chapter Two I summarized Hoover and Howard's distinction between traditional (attack-oriented) and critical dialogue. Critical Dialogue, they emphasize, assumes a multiplicity of perspectives and is embedded in an attempt to construct community and establish inclusive public space. In a complementary article entitled "Dialogue Across Differences: Continuing the Conversation,"[9] Burbules and Rice define public space as a location characterized by commitment to dialogue across differences. Burbules and Rice cite public schools as one very important place where this should be a goal.

> There must be some forums in which such dialogue across differences is valued, and in which it is pursued by participants in good faith, even in the face of difficulty and initial misunderstanding. We believe that educational contexts potentially provide one such forum. Public schools and universities are certainly no more free from social and political conflict and patterns of domination than are any other institutions, but they do generally espouse and frequently enact a commitment – particularly at the university level – to the value of communication across difference and the benefits of encountering new and challenging points of view.[10]

In contrast to claims about how anonymity eliminates the barriers that difference poses to inclusion, Burbules and Rice emphasize that it is the construction of difference and how differences are assigned meaning and practices of communication around them that minimizes or maximizes inclusion. Instead of finding ways to pretend that socially significant differences are not really there, a process which tends to reinforce hegemonic norms of universality, Burbules and Rice insist that sensitivity to differences that translates into inclusive interactive dispositions and skills is required. These authors provide some pointers as to the qualities of dialogue that contribute to inclusiveness.

> The success of dialogue across differences also depends on what we have called "communicative virtues" that help make dialogue possible and help sustain the dialogical relation over time. These virtues include tolerance, patience, respect for differences, a willingness to listen, the inclination to admit that one may be mistaken, the ability to reinterpret or translate one's own concerns in a way that makes them comprehensible to others, the self-imposition of restraint in order that others may "have a turn" to speak, and the disposition to express one's self honestly and sincerely. The possession of these virtues influences one's capacities both to express one's own beliefs, values, and feelings accurately, and to listen and to hear those of others.[11]

They go on to emphasize the relationship between communicative virtues and inclusivity in the educational process.

> The point of stressing the communicative virtues is not to advance a particular educational or political agenda over others, but rather to suggest the dispositions that seem necessary for promoting any open and serious discussion about such matters. If a tentative agreement about how we ought to proceed educationally is to be inclusive in any meaningful sense, then it will require dialogue expressive of the communicative virtues.[12]

Given the responsibility of public education to welcome/socialize students into citizenship, the educational system should ascribe first, to the goal of being genuinely public/inclusive itself, and second, to contributing to the development of more genuinely inclusive spaces throughout society by providing all of us with opportunities to develop inclusive behaviours and skills. Given the role of various technologies in restructuring our world (new information technologies, biotechnologies, etceteras), the mission of the public education system to contribute to more inclusive public spaces in society cannot be conceived of or actualized without the commitment to enable the citizenry to engage meaningfully in decisions about technology.

CONNECTION TO OLD VS. NEW PARADIGMS OF POST-SECONDARY TEACHING

Differences between old and new forms of pedagogy relate to notions of the public – survival of the fittest versus inclusion and the facilitation/development of multiple contributions. Traditional pedagogical approaches emphasized the teacher as knowledge broker and the student as receiver of knowledge. The work was about content mastery. The "new" pedagogy – ranging from critical pedagogy that emphasizes teaching and learning as embedded within relations of power to social constructivism with its focus on learning as an activity – emphasizes the student as learner in a social context and knowledge as produced within a social context. To date, this student-centred pedagogy seems to have been more thoroughly adopted at the elementary level where teachers are working to accommodate individual differences and build social systems.

Johnson et al. make a distinction between the "old" and "new" paradigms of teaching. The old paradigm of teaching, often referred to as the "transmission" approach is characterized by the assumption that student minds are like blank sheets of paper for instructors to write on; students are considered to be empty vessels waiting to be filled with knowledge by the instructor. It is assumed that knowledge is something possessed by those with credentials and that a competitive atmosphere is ideal for learning. The new paradigm, in contrast, recognizes limitations of the adversarial, competitive model of teaching and emphasizes the process of knowledge construction as a social process involving students and instructors. Knowledge construction is embedded within the broader social context. Johnson et al. emphasize that

> All of the above can only take place within a cooperative context.
> When students interact within a competitive context communication is
> minimized, misleading and false information is often communicated,
> helping is minimized and viewed as cheating, and classmates and faculty tend to be disliked and distrusted. Competitive and individualistic
> learning situations, therefore, discourage active construction of knowledge and the development of talent by isolating students and creating
> negative relationships among classmates and with instructors.[13]

Burbules and Rice's communicative virtues and the inclusive environment they foster are consistent with Johnson et al's emphasis on cooperation and interaction and stand in stark contrast to the adversarial norms of academic culture.[14]

Johnson et al's leadership in cooperative learning, I am convinced, is about the connection between learning and inclusion. Good pedagogy is increasingly about creating an inclusive public space in the classroom – characterized by the construction of knowledge in relationships – among students and between students and instructor. Instructional techniques that foster a climate of intimidation and competition, are increasingly being identified as impediments to the learning process.

TRYING IT OUT: SA 292

I recently taught a second year sociology course entitled "New Information Technology and Society."[15] A course of this nature was a first in the department and resulted from a proposal I had submitted. It was my intention to provide students (some with computer background, most without) with a structured forum within which to become familiar with developments in computer-based communications technologies and to critically explore the implications of these technologies. Typically, computer courses concentrate specifically on learning to use the technology, while courses about science and technology, philosophy of science, or gender and technology maintain an academic distance and refrain from engaging directly with the technology. My goal was to provide students with an opportunity to gain literacy *with* the technology and *about* the technology, by providing a course that combined a hands-on approach to the technology with a critical forum for assessing its embeddedness within a larger social context, its positive and negative implications, and instances of and opportunities for resistance.

The course was divided between time in the classroom and time in the lab. One of the assignments was the construction of a web page demonstrating knowledge of and interaction with course materials. The software for web page construction has, by this time, developed to the point where it is possible for students with little computer background to engage with the medium. Many of the resulting web pages were breathtaking in their creativity, beauty, and critical complexity. One of the most visually beautiful and critically provocative pages was constructed by a student who had no computer background whatsoever.

In lab sessions we explored the internet, at first in same-sex pairs, to gain familiarity with cyberspace rather than just talking about it in class. The buddy system was set up to emphasize the sharing of skills between and among students, in contrast to more typical patterns of isolation/competition. Research on gender and computing was a basis for placing students in same-sex pairs. The masculine bias of computing technology and gendered norms about entitlement and technological competence made it important for the women in the class, some of whom were unfamiliar with the technology and some of whom were very competent, to be paired at least in the beginning[16]. I selected the pairs with the aims of facilitating skill sharing and compatible communication styles in mind.

A key focus was the exploration of the role of information technologies in the construction of insiders and outsiders according to social, political and economic dimensions. This was combined with a practical pedagogical orientation towards an inclusive climate that informs my teaching in all contexts. Students and instructor made connections between discussions about the western public sphere in general, debates about the democratic potential of cyberspace, and our own efforts to create and maintain a welcoming climate for experimentation and for critical dialogue in our classroom and our lab.

Concrete steps aimed at creating a more inclusive climate in the classroom included generating and agreeing to a list of "Guidelines for Communication and Conduct."

SA 292 (January 1999)

GUIDELINES FOR COMMUNICATION AND CONDUCT

(subject to renegotiation at any time)

- listen while others are speaking
- avoid interrupting
- avoid background chatter
- respect the fact/expect others to have different opinions
- don't be afraid to disagree
- ask questions/encourage people to develop/communicate their ideas
- share the conversational space – avoid dominating discussions
- avoid jumping to conclusions about a person on the basis of a few of their ideas
- avoid negative/dismissive responses/body language

- be sensitive to different levels of ability
- all questions are relevant
- don't be afraid to pause/don't be afraid of silence
- avoid sharing unnecessarily gory details

I introduced the activity of creating a list of guidelines for the class by explaining my desire to have as many students as possible feel welcome to contribute to the conversation and by articulating the benefit that would be derived by hearing different perspectives. Students responded enthusiastically and thoughtfully in suggesting guidelines. Classroom and lab interactions were, to my knowledge, reasonably consistent with these guidelines. It is challenging to create a community in a 13 week semester and no doubt there were students who were reluctant to contribute to discussions, some tended to speak more than others, and there were times when I facilitated classroom or lab interaction without appropriate intention and critical-mindedness. As in all learning, though, our emphasis, both with the guidelines and the class and lab climate, was on learning/struggling to be more purposively inclusive, rather than in documenting our success or failure.

One of the consequences of using the buddy system in the lab right from the beginning, in combination with a group decision to bring in a CD boom box and play our favourite CDs while we worked, was the establishment of a very social, often festive atmosphere. Initially, I formally called for students to check in with their buddies periodically but before too long that interaction was spontaneous and frequent. There was a lot of physical movement within the lab, as students checked out what each other had found and sought each other out for assistance.

Be My Fag/Sa292 in the Chat Room

A significant moment occurred toward the end of our term when, at the suggestion of one of the students, we explored a chat room on *yahoo.com* as a group. We created our own room but did not make it private. Most of us made up names for ourselves and the style of communication was pretty silly and playful. Some of the comments in the chat room related to the selection of music currently being played and when one of the students took over as DJ (usually my role), there was widespread approval of his hip choices. Our new DJ was a popular openly gay man in the class and the ensuing dialogue in the chat room went something like this.

A: Ooooh, great tunes J.
S: Yeah, J, be mine.(female)
B: J says "but I'm a fag"
Z: J, be my fag.
A: No, J, be MY fag.

In another setting, with other people, a conversation like this could be highly homophobic and exclusive. In this setting, it was fun, irreverent, affectionate and celebratory of difference (queer positive).

In the middle of this conversation, a new "person" appeared in the space under the name "Carolina." It soon became apparent that "Carolina" was not a member of our class but had stumbled across our chat room in her wanderings through cyberspace. She announced her presence in the middle of our competition for J's affections by stating:

"Homosexuals suck"

One of our group responded: "Lots of people suck, if you're lucky." The group in the lab laughed. But Carolina could not have known that.

Carolina responded: "Are you all fags in here?"

Her response was a series of posts from many members of our group proudly proclaiming gay and lesbian identity. For example,

S: "yup, we're all fags and dykes, want to join us?"
A: "yup, I'm a fag"
D: "me too, I'm a fag."

Etceteras.

More class members asserted queer identity in addressing the intrusion of homophobia into our space. Carolina was not criticized or attacked: she met with a positive affirmation and celebration of queer identity, by both queer and not-so-queer members of our group alike.

Carolina left the chat room.

I was stunned. I knew I had witnessed something about social control in public space that was truly inspiring. Rather than "flame" Carolina and allow her homophobia to establish a hostile, polemic tone in the space, the group maintained a climate of fun and celebration while energetically protecting "our fag" and the inclusive nature of our little piece of cyberspace.

Freedom of Speech vs. Censorship/Freedom *To* versus Freedom *From*

Theoretical work received the same serious attention, in the same supportive environment. I shared my research on the public nature of cyberspace in general and my case study of *ncf.general*. This sparked a discussion that was framed, primarily by the students, in terms of the conflict between censorship and freedom of speech in public space. After hearing my summary of the dominant discourse in *ncf.general* emphasizing freedom of speech as the indicator of public space above all, and some very disturbing examples of racism, misogyny and homophobia on *ncf.general*, students nonetheless asserted the importance of freedom of speech above all else in determining the extent to which a space can be called public. They gave good reasons, citing the history of state censorship and its targets. Examples included the history of gays and lesbians and First Nations peoples being censored out of public space.

I tried to shift the conversation away from the polemic of state censorship versus the anything goes associated with freedom of speech by asking the class to try the following: First, consider the issue of public space in terms of the difference between emphasizing *freedom to* as opposed to *freedom from* in establishing inclusivity. I argued that the emphasis on freedom to creates an environment that can be so toxic and threatening as to de facto exclude all but the voices of exclusion and the truly thick-skinned. If we consider instead *freedom from* as an indicator of publicness we have a different situation. If participants are able to interact without being insulted or flamed, if racism, sexism, homophobia are discouraged, I argued that more people would feel welcome in the space and hence it would be more public. If quality of dialogue was aimed for, and voices preaching hatred were discouraged, the space would be more public. It would not mean there could not or would not be severe disagreements and conflicts; but the critical thinking steps aimed at encouraging genuine dialogue that I had outlined early in the semester (Burbules and Rice) would guide interaction in the space. Second, I asked the class to think of our classroom as public space and to make a comparison between discussions about the public sphere, whether in or out of cyberspace, and efforts we were making in our classroom to make it more inclusive. I acknowledged that much remained to be done in achieving greater inclusivity in our classroom (as I looked around the room and acknowledged to myself that several students rarely contributed to whole class discussions – although much of the small group work I had designed to increase participation was highly successful), but if we followed the freedom to rather than the freedom from consensus among the majority of students in the beginning of the discussion, we would not be having a discussion like this and we would not have been having anywhere near as much fun.

Students responded acknowledging the need to broaden the discussion of public space away from pro- versus anti-government interference and appreciation for efforts at inclusivity made in our class. In particular, they expressed gratitude for the comfortable environment and appreciated each other for being helpful in terms of skill-sharing, and for being receptive to different perspectives.

CONCLUSIONS FROM TRYING IT OUT

In our discussions of freedom of speech, censorship, and climate, we struggled with the issue of social control and policing. On a practical level, the classroom guidelines represented our efforts to establish parameters of acceptable behaviour in our interaction, or to render explicit our "communicative virtues". As a group we grappled theoretically with the concept of public space, and we modelled our "public" in the chat room with the individual/collective responses to homophobia representing some of those guidelines put into practice. Carolina was not attacked – her attacks on gay and lesbian identity were addressed with a celebratory response. There is no question that our group had the security of a queer positive environment within which to engage in this very non-violent form of social control of our little public space.

> Burbules and Rice claim that communicative virtues are only acquired in relation to communicative partners, and improved by practice. Thus to develop these virtues is to be drawn into certain kinds of communicative relationship: to become tolerant, patient, and respecting of others through association with people who are similarly disposed.[17]

In the chat room, the students' real world experiences influenced their cyberworld behaviour. They had knowledge of, and experience with critical dialogue, a relaxed and hospitable work environment, buddies, explicit guidelines of behaviour of their own design, expectation of and appreciation for the diversity within their group, a sense of camaraderie, and a sense of humour. These elements combined to enable them to respond non-violently to hatred expressed in public space. Moreover, the object of that hatred may have felt more secure because of safety in terms of numbers or in terms of widespread personal support.

Creating an hospitable climate with the intention, in turn, of creating an inclusive public, is no easy task, even in the intimate surround of a small classroom/lab. The challenge of constructing a public in cyberspace, without benefit of face-to-face engagement over time, shared responsibilities or hip music, is even more daunting. Early introductions of computers talked about the need for a balance between high tech and high touch. My experience with SA 292 convinces me that above all, constructing the public is neither typical nor accidental. Rather than assuming that the anonymity of cyberspace will promise inclusion, we must assume it will not. We must structure the social into relationships that are by definition remote; build explicit conditions for participation on the assumption that strangers do not arrive in the chat room with trust and suspended judgement; model and expect tolerance and respect; and assume and celebrate difference. Moreover, we must do these same things in our real world communities, and especially in our schools as they function as incubators for citizens who will need well developed communicative virtues as they move into various public spheres.

Critical pedagogy facilitates the development of a language of critical discourse. If we use it as a social force we may be able to foster a generation of technoliterate skeptics, equipping our society to engage critically with both the content and the consequences of new technologies. Support for this critical engagement is an important contribution educators can make to efforts to trouble boundaries between insiders and outsiders as society shifts and changes.

New technologies may ironically be influential because they bring with them to campus new resources and attention that may enable educators to engage critically about the social. Failure to engage critically will enable these emerging technologies to entrench outsider educational and social practices, diminishing both real and cyberpublics.

NOTES

[1] Donna Haraway, *Simians, Cyborgs and Women: The Reinvention of Nature.* (New York: Routledge, 1991), p. 163.

[2] Donna Haraway, *Simians, Cyborgs and Women: The Reinvention of Nature.* (New York: Routledge, 1991), p. 181.

[3] Donna Haraway, *Simians, Cyborgs and Women: The Reinvention of Nature.* (New York: Routledge, 1991), p. 154.

⁴ Heather Menzies. *Whose Brave New World: The Information Highway and the New Economy*. (Toronto: Between the Lines, 1996); Jeremy Rifkin. *The End of Work: the Decline of the Global Labour Force and the Dawn of the Post-Market Era*. (New York: Putnam, 1995).

⁵ Constance Penley and Andrew Ross, eds. *Technoculture*. Minneapolis: University of Minnesota Press, 1991.

⁶ Neil Postman. *Technopoly: The Surrender of Culture to Technology*. New York: Vintage Books, 1993, p. 20.

⁷ Neil Postman. *Technopology: The Surrender of Culture to Technology*. New York: Vintage Books, 1993, p. 18.

⁸ Jean Lave and Etienne Wenger, *Situated Learning: Legitimate Peripheral Participation*. (Cambridge: Cambridge University Press, 1991).

⁹ Nicholas Burbules and Suzanne Rice, "Dialogue Across Differences: Continuing the Conversation," in *Harvard Educational Review*. Vol. 61, No. 4, November 1991.

¹⁰ Nicholas Burbules and Suzanne Rice, "Dialogue Across Differences: Continuing the Conversation," in *Harvard Educational Review*. Vol. 61, No. 4, November 1991, p. 407.

¹¹ Nicholas Burbules and Suzanne Rice, "Dialogue Across Differences: Continuing the Conversation," in *Harvard Educational Review*. Vol. 61, No. 4, November 1991, p. 411.

¹² Nicholas Burbules and Suzanne Rice, "Dialogue Across Differences: Continuing the Conversation," in *Harvard Educational Review*. Vol. 61, No. 4, November 1991, p. 411.

¹³ David W. Johnson, Roger T. Johnson and Karl A. Smith. Active Learning: Cooperation in the College Classroom. (Edina, MN: Interaction, 1991), p. 1-11.

¹⁴ Nicholas Burbules and Suzanne Rice, "Dialogue Across Differences: Continuing the Conversation," in *Harvard Educational Review*. Vol. 61, No. 4, November 1991, p. 412.

¹⁵ SA 292, Department of Sociology and Anthroplogy, Simon Fraser University, Burnaby, B.C., January –April 1999.

¹⁶ Dale Spender, *Nattering on the Net: Women, Power and Cyberspace*. (Toronto: Garamond Press, 1995); Judy Wajcman, *Feminism Confronts Technology*. (University Park, PA: Pennsylvania State University, 1991).

¹⁷ Nicholas Burbules and Suzanne Rice, "Dialogue Across Differences: Continuing the Conversation," in *Harvard Educational Review*. Vol. 61, No. 4, November 1991, p. 411.

CHAPTER 5

Feminist Counterpublics

Given that public cyberspace is de facto exclusive, one might ask why so many writers (print-based and web-based) and activists concerned with inclusivity (whether they focus on matters relating to identity politics or education) would put so much time and energy into contesting its restrictive tendencies. For example, Jennifer Light wonders whether women should participate in *mixed* public spaces in cyberspace or if they would do better to create women-only public spaces.[1]

> Should women trying to degender the computer start with all-female groups or try to integrate themselves into mostly male groups? Should they allow men to participate in their discussions of women's issues?[2]

Some feminists dismiss the value of computer technology altogether, arguing that it is so inherently masculine and oppressive as to be unredeemable. Increasingly, however, this posture is being recognized not only as unrealistic, given the relentless extension of technology into all aspects of life, but also as unproductive. Penley and Ross are joined by Donna Haraway in cautioning against taking an anti-technological posture. In her highly influential "Manifesto for Cyborgs," Haraway agues for problematizing the boundaries between dichotomies traditional to a Cartesian worldview, such as nature/artifice, woman/man, animal/human, etceteras[3]. In a subsequent interview by Penley and Ross, Haraway warns that

We can't afford the "one-dimensional man" critique of technological rationality, which is to say, we can't turn scientific discourses into the Other, and make them into the enemy, while still contesting what nature will be for us. We have to engage in those terms of practice, and resist the temptation to remain pure.[4]

Moreover, there are several examples whereby women have had some success in "feminizing" a technology through use in unintended ways. The widespread installation of the telephone, for example, while intended primarily for the benefit of business interests, became a means for women to maintain social networks from the "privacy" of their homes.[5] The way in which a technology is actually used can potentially subvert the intentions of its designers and marketers and achieve other objectives instead.

Feminist analyses of the implications of cyberspace for the traditional western mind/body dualism are important. After all, women's bodies constitute a central site of struggle and conflict between women and men, women and the state, women and consumer culture. As Haraway remarks, "bodies are maps of power and identity."[6] The tension between embodiment and much computing culture has powerful implications for the ways in which women experience cyberspace and for the ways in which the culture of cyberspace is produced and reproduced. Many gender researchers argue that women and men are generally socialized into different patterns of communication, with women's communicative behaviours emphasizing the social and connection and men's focusing more on skill and mastery[7]. The different ways in which men and women reproduce and are reproduced by culture translates into different relationships with/uses of technology. For example, commenting on the use of the Internet by female engineers, Ellen Ullman observes that

> being women as well as engineers, most of us can communicate on multiple channels. We use the Internet as a tool, like the phone or the fax, a way to transmit news and make appointments.[8]

She refers to this use of multiple channels for communication as "codeswitching" and suggests that this very female facility makes online participation for women less appealing.

> Maybe this is why there are fewer of us on-line: We already have company. For the men, their on-line messages *are* their relationships. They

seem content in the net's single channeledness, relations wrapped in the envelope of technology: one man, one wire.[9]

Perhaps it is this very capacity for codeswitching and the valuation of technology as tool rather than as ideology, to paraphrase John Rawlston Saul,[10] that may enable feminists to address the tension between embodiment and computing culture by grounding computer-based communication in social relations that privilege embodiment.

There are very practical reasons for encouraging feminist involvement in the creation of public cyberspaces and participation within public cyberspace. As Spender emphasizes, the risks of remaining outside this new medium are considerable:

> If computer competence were an optional leisure skill, or just another means of collecting your mail, the gender gap might be merely a fascinating phenomenon. But there is nothing optional any longer about computer involvement. The electronic medium is the way we now make sense of the world, and this is why women have to be full members of the computer culture. Women have to take part in making and shaping that cyber-society, or else they risk becoming the outsiders: they will be the information-poor, as they were for so long after the introduction of print.[11]

"Being the information-poor" relegates women, and other "others" for that matter, to a limited place in the economy, in the community, in the society. The information-poor are objects, rather than subjects. Their participation is limited, their futures determined by others. Strategies for feminist involvement in writing public cyberspace need to be developed. Exploration of *ncf.general* as a particular "public" site in cyberspace enables me to offer some suggestions in this regard.

Cyberspace provides a platform, and opportunities for people to speak to audiences larger than they would find in other mediums. Is this a good thing? As much as we explore opportunities for feminist/progressive creation and resistance within these new spaces, we must acknowledge that possibilities are provided for increased communication and exchange of information for conservative organizations and hatemongers.

The social impact of changing technologies has always been complex. Changes associated with computer technology are so rapid as to make attempts at understanding very difficult and prediction unreliable.

Mander encourages us to ask not what technology can do for us personally, but what technology can do for those in power[12]. Ursula Franklin extends this question beyond a merely defensive posture by suggesting that

> it may be wise, when communities are faced with new technological solutions to existing problems, to ask what these techniques may *prevent* and not only check what the techniques promise to *do*.[13]

Franklin provides an example of the way technologies prevent action. She points out that "tools often redefine a problem" and she traces the history of speed limits, originally instituted to enhance safety. The tool of the radar trap was introduced to police the speed limit, shifting the emphasis from common safety to individual deterrence. The next technology, the "fuzz buster", was designed in turn to avoid the radar trap, causing

> The common problem of road safety [to be] transformed into the private problem of fines and demerits and into a technological cat-and-mouse game. One might say that the technological tools designed to establish random criminality have prevented the development of techniques to establish collectively safe driving patterns.

Franklin continues, highlighting the important contextual complexity of technology:

> What needs to be emphasized is that technologies are developed and used within a particular social, economic, and political context. They arise out of a social structure, they are grafted on to it, and they may reinforce it or destroy it, often in ways that are neither foreseen nor foreseeable.[14]

Inquiry needs to occur, therefore, especially into the limitations that result from the way in which the technologies combine with social action to create cyberspaces: what do the technologies enable and what do the technologies prevent? While the amount of critical work on cyberspace is increasing[15], insufficient attention has been paid to the ways in which text-based sites in cyberspace produce and reproduce communities of practice, in short, to the ways in which the public is written. In identifying some of the limitations and/or patterns of interaction common to these new spaces, opportunities for resistance may be revealed.

Of particular value in exploring feminist possibilities in the new public spaces fostered by computer-based communications technologies is an understanding of the existence of a multiplicity of public spaces and potential for further expansion. Surpassing critiques of the unitary liberal democratic public sphere, increasing attention is being paid to the existence and importance of multiple public spheres. Part of the construction of the public sphere as universal in liberal democratic theory forecloses an acknowledgment of the multiplicity of public spaces. But an acknowledgment of the limited extent to which the official public sphere is genuinely public, that is, inclusive, has created opportunities for understanding "other" limited spheres as public in a similar sense. For example, Robbins notes the "public" spaces peculiar to children.[16] Feminist organizing has deliberately created feminist public spaces that parallel and contest the "general public." Habermas, with his investment in the bourgeois public sphere as the peak of democracy and hence the central project of its revitalization,[17] typifies this unified framework. Radical democratic theorists such as Laclau and Mouffe and feminist scholars such as Fraser challenge the notion of the liberal democratic sphere, not only in terms of its universality and hence inclusive character, but in terms of its singularity. They argue that public spaces are multiple and, as Fraser notes, they exist in particular contexts:

> history records that members of subordinate social groups - women, workers, peoples of colour, and gays and lesbians - have repeatedly found it advantageous to constitute alternative publics.[18]

Fraser further describes these subaltern counterpublics as

> parallel discursive arenas where members of subordinated social groups invent and circulate counterdiscourses, so as to formulate oppositional interpretations of their identities, interests, and needs.[19]

These counterpublics play an important role in the stratified societies of the West in that they allow for the consolidation of identity and regroupment while supporting more effective efforts for inclusion in the larger society. Fraser has pointed to the hisory of "caucusing" as an effective strategy for marginalized groups in esablishing efficacy in the public sphere.

STRATEGIES FOR FEMINIST CONTESTATION AND RE-WRITING OF THE PUBLIC IN CYBERSPACE

Given the increasing significance of on-line/web-based communication, creating more inclusive public cyberspaces is an important component of social change movements that seek a more equitable distribution of wealth and power in society. As Mitchell reminds us, however:

> Inclusion of more and varied groups of people into the public sphere has only been won through constant social struggle.[20]

Deliberate and strategic political action is required if public cyberspace is to come closer to achieving the normative impulse for inclusion underlying ideologies of the public.

Public spaces are constructed and increasingly, these settings are cybernetically fostered. Feminist involvement in the social conversation *and* in the technological conversation is therefore crucial. As Robbins emphasizes, these conversations and the construction of public space are ongoing:

> no sites are inherently or eternally public. The lines between public and private are perpetually shifting, as are the tactical advantages and disadvantages of finding oneself on one side or the other.[21]

Public cyberspaces will be constructed with or without feminist input; norms and sanctions establishing boundaries between insiders and outsiders and with respect to quality of dialogue will be developed with or without feminist input. In Chapters Two and Three, I found that the norms and sanctions and the quality of dialogue produced an exclusive climate. Unless contested by feminist/progressive voices, this is likely to continue.

As emphasized in Chapters Two and Three, the exclusion of voices, content, and participatory styles, makes *ncf.general* an unappealing and significantly limited "public" space. However, if the understandable feminist revulsion results in a boycott of cyberspace, it may have the risky consequence of ensuring that the exclusiveness of public cyberspace becomes a self-fulfilling prophecy. Without feminist and progressive contestation, the more inhospitable these spaces are bound to become, and the greater the likelihood that they will be left to the likes of people like Elliott D and Dustin P. As Joan Baez once reminded an audience, "Don't blame Ronald Reagan - it's not *his* fault he's President."

The particular narrowness of cyberpublics may be a result of the restriction of social interaction to text, therefore grounding cyberpublics in embodied social relations may be the most important contribution that feminists can be make. Ullman's characterization of women's multichannelled communicative style as "codeswitching" is promising in this regard. By highlighting issues related to embodiment in cyberspace and/or integrating interaction in public cyberspaces with social interaction in other mediums, whether face-to-face or technologically fostered in other ways (telephone, television, radio, for example), feminists have the potential to counter the tendency to glorify the disembodying capabilities of cyberspace with a more humanizing influence. In this way, feminists may achieve greater inclusivity and enrichment in public cyberspaces.

In the first place, issues of access need to be more formally addressed. As such, linkages to larger projects for social, economic and political equity and justice need to be made so that the factors that make cyberspace an elite space are at least somewhat mitigated.[22] In the second place, public cyberspace needs to be claimed and transformed.

The possibilities for feminist action in here are considerable. However, as I mentioned in Chapter One and in the beginning of this Chapter, feminists are likely to wonder, at least on an individual level if not on a collective level, if activism in cyberspace is warranted or likely to be rewarding. Given the overwhelming tasks for feminist activists in other social arenas, encouragement to contest public cyberspaces may not be well received.

The reasons I have listed, in Chapter One and here, for feminist engagement with these new social spaces emphasize both the value of feminist input as early on in the process as possible, and the awareness that these spaces will be constructed with or without feminist input. While "climate" and "space" may seem "natural" or "external" conditions in cyberspace, my research highlights the ways in which they are actually socially constructed. Feminists have made gains by drawing attention to particularity and the falseness of universal posturing. But such gains are never permanent; the spheres in which they are achieved change and new spheres that may or may not reflect these gains are constantly emerging. Feminists and other activists may lament being called upon to "reinvent the wheel" but any assumption that gains in social struggle are permanent is naive and historically unsupported.

Computer-based communications technologies are neither neutral nor likely to disappear any time soon. Their impact is widespread. We have only to think of the already visible implications of new technologies for the global economy, most notably in terms of the globalization of labour.

While on an individual level feminists appropriately gravitate towards activism in spheres that are immediately meaningful to us, the feminist movement as a whole cannot ignore the implications of computer-based technologies on women and gender relations in society. Feminists must continue to pose alternatives to the ideology of individualized freedom of speech, so clearly deleterious to diverse participation in *ncf.general*. As new social spheres emerge, new forms of feminist contestation must emerge with them. Spender's words are worth repeating:

> Women have to take part in making and shaping that cyber-society, or else they risk becoming outsiders . . . [23]

Feminists have experienced outsider status in public spaces far too often to be complacent as new spaces are constructed around old norms of exclusion.

That the emergence of this new social sphere places heavy burdens on an already embattled feminist movement is clear; that ignoring it is not an option is also clear. Like the suffragettes who fought so hard to ensure that women could participate at least nominally in the public spheres of western democracies, it is probable that in pioneering feminist scholarship in the area of gender and technology Sally Hacker, Cynthia Cockburn, Donna Haraway, and many others were (and are) overwhelmed at times by the amount of energy required. Fortunately, they were able to find resources sufficient to the task and their insights provide feminists working on issues related to gender and technology today with powerful tools and an encouraging reality check with respect to the masculinism of technology and power.

A key outcome of any successful feminist action in contesting and re-writing the public in cyberspace is the inclusion in the discourse of the public of an understanding of the way in which climate effects opportunities for participation. While individual efforts in specific sites in cyberspace may expand the horizons of some participants and/or provide individuals with a feeling of integrity for not having remained silent in the face of discourses of marginalization and hatred, individuals acting alone will not transform public cyberspace. Solitary acts on the part of feminists and pro-feminist men, while not irrelevant, unless combined with collective effort will not go far beyond ineffective martyrdom. Feminist efforts to re-write the public in cyberspace to allow for greater inclusiveness need to be collectively organized and strategically well thought out. It is easy to see how quickly progressive attempts to transform public cyberspace would fizzle out as individuals involved become burned out by the incredible density of opposition.

Models for successful feminist contestation of cyberspace exist in both the Black Civil Rights Movement of the 1950s and 1960s[24] and in feminist organizing from the 1960s on.[25] The lunch counter sit-in practice was common during the civil rights movement and it was successful. It challenged the mainstream public to enforce the laws of segregation while denying the legitimacy of these laws, and it had a certain practical appeal while providing an opportunity to make a powerful moral and political statement. The denial of public space to Black Americans[26] amounted to a denial of resources and opportunities. Not only did Black Americans fight against the *principle* of exclusion but against the *practice* of exclusion as they demanded their right to walk into a public restaurant and sit down and eat.

I expect that the mere principle of public cyberspace's exclusiveness may be insufficient to inspire effective feminist action. However, practical reasons for claiming public cyberspace are becoming increasingly apparent.

Feminist contestation of exclusive practices in supposedly public spaces and strategies designed for achieving social change have been firmly grounded, since the 1970s, in a parallel strategy of organizing feminist counterpublics, as Fraser has observed, and in problematizing the exclusiveness of supposedly public spaces. Combining the strategic tactics that proved so effective in the Black Civil Rights Movement with this parallel strategy of claiming and re-writing public cyberspace has significant promise.

Feminist on-line organizing may coincide with off-line organizing or it may take place entirely on-line. Either way, it should not detract from the awareness that the construction of social reality in cyberspace is as "real" as in off-line social spaces. We have observed the complexity of the way in which the public is "written" in cyberspace, through the articulation of values and ideology and through the collapsing of articulation/behaviour. In off-line social settings, the public is articulated and the public is behaved. The technology of cyberspace does not alter these components of social behaviour; rather, it typically collapses them into text/symbols/images and increasingly sounds. Feminists organize to contest exclusive tendencies in a number of social spaces and its is important that cyberspaces be added to the list. Ideally, feminists will claim public cyberspace as a useful tool for organizing around issues in both on-line and off-line locations.

FEMINIST ACTIVITY IN CYBERSPACE

Feminist activity and the creation of positive images of women and computing on line is occurring – with impressive creativity, networking, and resistance to sexism on the web and the sexism of much of computing culture.[27] Numerous organizations with on- and off-line components aimed at providing women with resources for engaging with and about new information technologies have emerged, in North America and throughout the world.[28] A visit to several sites on the World Wide Web reveals the power of this web-like metaphor and matrix for social and political activity by women.

A recent exploration began with River Ginchild's web page entitled *Digital Sojourn* at *www.digitalsojourn.orglriver.html*. In an interview with *Processed Lives* contributor Wakeford, Ginchild explains that her web page is "named after human rights advocate Sojourner Truth [and] focuses on increasing the participation of people of African descent in computer-mediated communication."[29] By pointing and clicking on the *Digital Sojourn* web page I can travel to other web pages produced by women with similar or related goals. One of these links is to Wakeford's *Octavia Project*, a page designed to provide women in the United Kingdom with a set of resources on gender and technology on the Web.[30] Following the links provided on both these pages propels me into an endless world of feminist activism and community. As with the *Octavia Project*, many of these pages relate directly to issues of access and participation in cyberspace.

Another web session begins at Gentech, a feminist web page originating in Vancouver, British Columbia at *www.educ.sfu.ca/gentech*. This page is dedicated to issues and resources relating to gender and information technology. Along with information about and opportunities to participate in the authors' research, this page provides links and information on web sites dedicated to women and women's issues, health and bodies, women in science and technology, and information about university courses relating to women/gender, science and technology.

Another one of these feminist spaces is *Virtual Sisterhood* at *www.igc.apc.org/vsister*.

> Virtual Sisterhood coordinates and organizes connections to women's
> groups and activities, and provides links between activist groups and

social forums as well as an on-line periodical, *Seachange*. Information is available in a variety of languages, and women Web author volunteers establish sites which host women's groups from all over the world.[31]

Virtual Sisterhood, a cybernetically housed in WomensNet, provides a webring of pages by women designed to

> create and facilitate a global network of women committed to enhancing their own and other women's activism through effective use of electronic communications. The network prioritizes inclusion and empowerment of women of color, immigrant and refugee women, low-income women, lesbians, women from the Global South, older women, young women, women with disabilities, rural women and women from other communities, which have traditionally had little or no access to or control of electronic communications technology.[32]

By selecting "Random Site" on the Virtual Sisterhood's opening home page, I am treated to a selection of women's pages on the Web ring. On one journey, I am greeted first with

Welcome to jonnie's Breakfast (or anytime) Reading Page
<Picture>Breakfast (or Anytime) Reading . . .
This web page features information and contacts of women/lesbians and gays, articles and links to other lesbian and gay positive pages and resources including community newspapers and lists of banned books. Jonnie also includes pictures of herself and her friends.

Back to the Virtual Sisterhood Webring for another point and click at the random site button... For the next hour I visit pages including Woman Motorist, a page featuring car reviews and a shopping and maintenance guide, the Italian Federation of Business and Professional Women, an international networking page, and LCDV, a lesbian page designed to build community in the southern Pennsylvania, Delaware, and southern New Jersey region. All these sites feature point and click links to sites the authors consider related, interesting, or relevant. As Wakeford says,

> Connections cross-cut each other with multiple routes for getting from one page to another, adding complexity to the networks. Frequently they also encompass a convention of cooperation and sharing of technological skills between women which is related by some to previous projects of political networking among women.[33]

Wakeford goes on to quote from a Women'sSpace web page (Volume 1, No. 3):

> There is a spirit of generosity amongst sisters in cyberspace which reminds us of the early days of the Women's Liberation movement. Networking, activism, and support are interwoven as we push ourselves to learn to work with the new electronic tools we are encountering. Together we anticipate a future where growing numbers of women can access and use the global connections to promote women's equality.[34]

I am reminded of the fable "Six Degrees of Separation" by the connectivity that characterizes a seemingly endless volume of women's/feminist web pages. The long tradition of feminist networking is elevated about metaphor[35] in the web of activity in cyberspace.

Unlike *ncf.general*, a number of web-based discussion sites require participants to adhere to a more extensive code of conduct aimed, at least in principle, at establishing and maintaining a climate conducive to broad participation. These include the San Francisco-based *Well* documented in Howard Rheingold's *Virtual Community*, perhaps one of the largest and more durable sites in North America. Amazon City is a specifically feminist site. This page is affiliated with a larger cyberorganization called herspace: "the network for evolving women." Amazon City aims at providing a site for community formation, and hence a place where issues of inclusivity can be examined. The site opens with the following statement:

AMAZON CITY: Where she is the revolution
YOUR MISSION: OVERTHROW gender stereotypes
                EMPOWER women
                HAVE FUN

I can become a citizen of Amazon City, whether I am female, male, or undetermined. This citizenship entitles me to participate in the life of the community – including conversations in the commons and in Amazon City Café. Unlike the norms of anything goes with the exception of the most severe profanity that characterizes *ncf.general*, Amazon city citizenship requires agreement to follow city ordinances that emphasize civility and respect. Sexual harassment and identity-based attacks on individuals are specifically prohibited. Violation of these ordinances may result in the revoking of citizenship by the page's author.

In a brief review of conversations in progress at this site, I observed a quality of dialogue that emphasized responsiveness to the ideas of others and respect in the face of disagreement. For example, in a conference topic entitled "sexuality," an area of discussion in *ncf.general* that was guaranteed to be "hot," I found considerable disagreement about fundamental as opposed to socially constructed differences between men and women and some expressions of irritation at the way in which others expressed their views. But these expressions of disagreement and irritation were not characterized by personal attacks or insults. And in stark contrast to the conversations relating to categories of identity in *ncf.general*, I found numerous examples of responsiveness to the comments of others. For example, one poster responds to another's criticism by stating the following: "Once again I will graciously accept your criticism and I will not deny straying into the realm of emotionally driven debate..." Conversations about "hot topics" in this space are characterized by a significant degree of critical dialogue. In this sense, and perhaps because of the emphasis on civility, mutual respect and prohibition of identity-based insults or attacks, there are several indications that Amazon City is more genuinely public than *ncf.general*. This is but one example of feminist activity in constructing more inclusive (and hence more genuinely public) social spaces.

RECOMMENDATIONS

An analysis of the gendered character of computer technologies could lead to a dismissal of technologies in general. However, this is neither practical nor warranted. Feminism and technologies need not be essentially antipathetic. While Hacker remarks that women and workers are considered "bad" "if they take things into their own hands", the pressure to use technologies appropriately reveals that meaningful opportunities for unintentional use need to be explored and that opportunities for resistance do exist. After all, many forms of resistance have historically taken existing technologies and subverted them to highly different ends. Feminists should be practical enough to exploit these opportunities. Resistance to increasing domination along lines of historically constructed "difference" necessarily involves engagement with the technologies that threaten to construct us just as much as these technologies are constructed by us. Feminist action should be governed not only by principle but by what is useful and valuable to those involved. The opportunities for dissemination of information available in public cyberspace have practical appeal for feminists and other progressive social movements (and of course, for conservative/far right organizations as well).

I suggest that feminist efforts at re-writing public cyberspace begin with the following:

- establishment or utilization of feminist counterpublics, whether on-line or off-line, for strategic planning, support and for their own sake;
- identification and feminist colonization of so-called public sites whose exclusive tendencies need to be resisted. I am encouraging feminist cybergyrrlla action to claim the space by simply picking up on de facto entitlement and modelling alternative modes of interaction.

A key tactic involves following in the footsteps of the civil rights activists in their lunch counter campaign and contesting the space by literally *claiming the space*. Feminists can use the space for the benefit of the feminist action group involved, whether this be through a dissemination of information, discussion of issues of interest and importance, or whatever. What is claimed to be public space has historically been the space that a particular group has claimed and designated as public. The simple action of using the space *as if it were yours* to begin with subverts the assumptions relating to who it belongs to. Claiming the space in this way contests its exclusive character and begins the transformative process. Refusing to be bullied is an important form of political action but it requires a pro-active complement. Re-writing the public space involves modeling an alternative. This involves articulating and actualizing a discourse of the public, with its attendant norms and sanctions, that reflects the principles of critical as opposed to traditional dialogue. This approach has three parts: 1) formally articulating a discourse of the public that problematizes a hostile climate and the way in which norms and sanctions are used to police the subject so as to limit opportunities for participation; 2) modeling an alternative and more inclusive public by consistently avoiding flaming and polemical discussions and by refusing to engage with individuals who continue to use a traditional argumentative style; and 3) ensuring that actual policing and the ongoing construction and deconstruction of norms and sanctions is a collective responsibility aimed at expanding inclusiveness.

The opportunity for feminist contestation and re-writing of the public in cyberspace that is not available in off-line public spaces is for the creation of a parallel counterpublic rather than a sub-altern counterpublic. Cyberspace provides feminists with unique opportunities for establishing visible feminist publics, for creating feminist spaces without "going away" from the "general" public space. Historically, feminists and other marginalized groups have caucused or formed subaltern counterpublics to consolidate political power, enabling them to participate more effectively in "mixed" publics. This has been necessary because in these mixed settings, women who do speak up are interrupted, talked over or ignored and topics of concern to women are either ignored or addressed in a limited way. As a result, women have been denied the opportunity commonly available to men to interact *with each other* in public spaces, and have had to go elsewhere.

A critical mass of feminist and progressive participants engaged in an organized attempt to contest the exclusive nature of and re-write the public in a specific site in cyberspace has the capacity to occupy public space in a way that is unprecedented off-line. The ability to ignore participants who contribute to a hostile climate without having to "wait" for them to finish speaking while continuing both to model and use an alternative cyberpublic right in the middle of a mainstream public, is unique to cyberspace. Women's caucuses provide a basic model of climate control but such control is achieved through (hotly contested) separation from the main group. Participation in the main group is enhanced through the acquisition of skills and confidence and the development of solidarity around issues of particular concern to women in the caucus, away from the group as a whole.

In cyberspace, an effective strategy for challenging the public takes one step further the notion of the women's caucus as empowering its members to change the larger context. The necessarily separatist off-line subaltern counterpublic serves as the basis for organizing the contestation of the mainstream cyberpublic but gives way to a parallel structure on-line.

It would be inaccurate to suggest that such a parallel public is an entirely new phenomenon. Many groups have communicated with each other without withdrawing from the larger group. But this was only made possible by ensuring that the larger group was either unaware that such communication was occurring or incapable of understanding it. For example, gay men developed ways of identifying themselves to each other without others being aware; the dialect of American slaves allowed them to communicate with each other without being understood by their masters. But the establishment of a parallel public visible to participants in the public at large is especially powerful because it models an alternative.

CONCLUSION

Resistance to increasing domination along lines of historically constructed "difference" necessarily involves engagement with the technologies that threaten to construct us just as much as these technologies are constructed by us. Feminist and other radical voices must push for meaningful inclusion in the discursive processes by which technologically-mediated social relations are fostered. As much as there is a history of technology embedded in relations of domination, there is a history of subversion and resistance through uses that were not intended by the designers of the technology. Heather Menzies describes the information highway as "a restructuring agent."[36] Social restructuring is an ongoing process, containing opportunities for resistance and pro-activity. Feminist technoscepticism offers us the tools to participate critically.

NOTES

[1] Jennifer S. Light, "The Digital Landscape: New Space for Women?" in *Gender, Place and Culture*, Vol. 2, No. 2, 1995, pp. 133-146.

[2] Jennifer S. Light, "The Digital Landscape: New Space for Women?" in *Gender, Place and Culture*, Vol. 2, No. 2, 1995, p. 141.

[3] Donna Haraway, *Simians, Cyborgs, and Women: The Reinvention of Nature*. (New York: Routledge, 1991).

[4] Constance Penley and Andrew Ross, "Interview with Donna Haraway," in *Technoculture*. (Minneapolis: University of Minnesota Press, 1991), p. 5.

[5] Judy Wajcman, *Feminism Confronts Technology*. (University Park, PA: Pennsylvania State University, 1991).

[6] Donna Haraway, *Simians, Cyborgs, and Women: The Reinvention of Nature*. (New York: Routledge, 1991), p. 180.

[7] Judy Wajcman, *Feminism Confronts Technology*. (University Park, PA: Pennsylvania State University, 1991).

[8] Ellen Ullman, "Come in CQ," in *Wired Women*, Lynn Cherny and Elizabeth Reba Weise, eds. (Seattle: Seal Press, 1996), p. 10.

[9] Ellen Ullman, "Come in CQ," in *Wired Women*, Lynn Cherny and Elizabeth Reba Weise, eds. (Seattle: Seal Press, 1996), p. 10.

[10] John Rawlston Saul. *The Unconscious Civilization*. (Concord, Ontario: House of Anansi Press, 1995).

[11] Dale Spender, *Nattering on the Net: Women, Power and Cyberspace.* (Toronto: Garamond Press, 1995), p. 168.

[12] Jerry Mander, *In the Absence of the Sacred: the Failure of Technology and the Survival of the Indian Nations.* (San Francisco: Sierra Club Books, 1991).

[13] Ursula Franklin, *The Real World of Technology.* (Concord, Ontario: House of Anansi Press, 1990), p. 57.

[14] Ursula Franklin, *The Real World of Technology.* (Concord, Ontario: House of Anansi Press, 1990), p. 52.

[15] Dale Spender, *Nattering on the Net: Women, Power and Cyberspace.* Toronto: Garamond Press, 1995; Heather Menzies, Whose Brave New World: The Information Highway and the New Economy. (Toronto: Between the Lines, 1996).

[16] Bruce Robbins, "Introduction: The Public as Phantom," in *The Phantom Public Sphere,* Bruce Robbins, ed. (Minneapolis: University of Minnesota Press).

[17] Jurgen Habermas, *The Structural Transformation of the Public Sphere.* (Cambridge, Massachusetts: M.I.T. Press, 1969).

[18] Nancy Fraser, "Rethinking the Public Sphere: A contribution to the Critique of Actually Existing Democracy, in *The Phantom Public Sphere,* Bruce Robbins, ed. (Minneapolis: University of Minnesota Press, 1993), p. 14.

[19] Nancy Fraser, "Rethinking the Public Sphere: A contribution to the Critique of Actually Existing Democracy, in *The Phantom Public Sphere,* Bruce Robbins, ed. (Minneapolis: University of Minnesota Press, 1993), p. 14.

[20] Don Mitchell, "The End of Public Space? People's Park, Definitions of the Public, and Democracy," in *Annals of the Association of American Geographers,* 85(1), 1995, p. 116.

[21] Bruce Robbins, "Introduction: The Public as Phantom," in *The Phantom Public Sphere,* Bruce Robbins, ed. (Minneapolis: University of Minnesota Press, 1993), p. xv.

[22] Cheris Kramarae (1988), Dale Spender, (1995), and Cherny and Weise (1996).

[23] Dale Spender, *Nattering on the Net: Women, Power and Cyberspace.* (Toronto: Garamond Press, 1995), p. 168.

[24] Aldon D. Morris, *The Origins of the Civil Rights Movement: Black Communities Organizing for Change.* (New York: MacMillan, 1984).

[25] Jo Freeman, ed. *Women: A Feminist Perspective.* (Palo Alto, California: Mayfield Publishing, 1975).

[26] The use of the descriptive term "Black Americans" in this instance is intended to be historically specific rather than a display of ignorance about the currently more appropriate designator "African-Americans."

[27] Nina Wakeford. "Networking Women and Grrrls with Information/Communication Technology: surfing tales of the world wide web," in *Processed*

Lives, Jennifer Terry and Melodie Calvert, eds. (London and New York: Routledge, 1997), p. 61

[28] Additional examples include FeMiNa (*http://www.femina.com*); Wired Woman Society of Canada (*http://www.wiredwoman.com*);

[29] Nina Wakeford. "Networking Women and Grrrls with Information/Communication Technology: surfing tales of the world wide web," in *Processed Lives*, Jennifer Terry and Melodie Calvert, eds. (London and New York: Routledge, 1997), p. 58.

[30] Nina Wakeford. "Networking Women and Grrrls with Information/Communication Technology: surfing tales of the world wide web," in *Processed Lives*, Jennifer Terry and Melodie Calvert, eds. (London and New York: Routledge, 1997), p. 52.

[31] Nina Wakeford. "Networking Women and Grrrls with Information/Communication Technology: surfing tales of the world wide web," in *Processed Lives*, Jennifer Terry and Melodie Calvert, eds. (London and New York: Routledge, 1997), p. 59.

[32] Virtual Sisterhood, *WomensNet@IGC*, June 5, 1998.

[33] Nina Wakeford. "Networking Women and Grrrls with Information/Communication Technology: surfing tales of the world wide web," in *Processed Lives*, Jennifer Terry and Melodie Calvert, eds. (London and New York: Routledge, 1997), p. 60.

[34] in Nina Wakeford. "Networking Women and Grrrls with Information/ Communication Technology: surfing tales of the world wide web," in *Processed Lives*, Jennifer Terry and Melodie Calvert, eds. (London and New York: Routledge, 1997), p. 60.

[35] Donna Haraway, *Simians, Cyborgs, and Women: The Reinvention of Nature*. (New York: Routledge, 1991).

[36] Heather Menzies, *Whose Brave new World? The Information Highway and the New Economy*, (Toronto: Between the Lines: 1996).

CHAPTER 6

Public Technologies

In the Concise Oxford Dictionary, technology is narrowly defined as follows:

> "(Science of) practical or industrial art(s); ethnological study of development of such arts; application of science"[1]

This definition is very hard-ware, or even soft-ware oriented. "Technological," may also be defined more broadly as "systematic treatment."[2] Ursula Franklin defines technology as less about things and more about social practice and processes, and by so doing, creates space to shift the focus from the computers and software that facilitate cyberspace to its more complex social context and components. In a visit to my SA 292 class, the author Heather Menzies made a distinction between descriptions of the postindustrial age as "information society" where technology predominates and people disappear altogether and the description of our course, Information Technology *and* Society. The society is not the product of the technology.

I began my investigation of the inclusive tendencies of public cyberspaces with a scepticism based on mistrust of all claims to universalism and neutrality, as well as specific awareness of the exclusive tendencies of both the western public sphere and powerful technologies. I did find evidence in *ncf.general* that cyberspace is an elite space that parallels non-computer-based social spaces in patterns of exclusion and inequality. I found that without deliberate attention to the ways in which quality of dialogue produces a hostile or a welcoming climate, exclusive tenden-

cies are likely to prevail. And finally, I found that sites that define themselves as public in terms of guaranteeing freedom of expression (the *freedom to* emphasis as opposed to *freedom from*) tend to produce freedom
for a tiny minority. As Dale Spender puts it,

> At the moment online it looks like a men's changing room at a football
> match. There are all these men standing there at the door saying `you
> can come in if you want to, and you can take it.' You'd be bloody stupid
> as a woman to go in there. You're not physically barring people, but the
> sense of it being pissed-on male territory is obvious.[3]

My research on *ncf.general* provides a brief snapshot of a site in cyberspace that is characterized by the kind of norms of publicness
Spender decries. While this site alone provides insufficient evidence to
make reliable generalizations about the public nature of cyberspace, the
well documented impact of polemic and flaming-style interactions on
participation in real world publics suggests that assumptions of an inclusive cyberpublic should be examined carefully.

In Chapter One, I presented evidence to suggest that these promises
of technology are largely mythic. The promises of neutrality and universality do not pan out historically and the masculine bias of computing
technology and culture and the false promises attended to disembodiment maintain technology's exclusive character. The fundamental error
is that of seeking a solution to the challenge of creating inclusive public
spheres in the wrong place. The emphasis placed by internet utopians on
the opportunities provided by computer hardware and software for expanding public space is misplaced; the technologies of the public that
need to be developed relate to patterns and practices of *social* interaction.

Hoover and Howard provide some basic technologies of the public
with their distinction between traditional dialogue and critical dialogue.
Burbules and Rice add their insights about the specific "communicative
virtues" that are essential for inclusive interaction. These technologies
aim at improving the quality of dialogue and hence inclusiveness are
consistent with the climate metaphor that has been utilized to raise
awareness around obstacles to participation and inclusion beyond de
facto attendance at post-secondary institutions.

In text-based cyberspace, quality of dialogue *IS* climate. In the material world of physical space, extremes of climate attack the body in the
form of frostbite or sunburn; in the "metaphoric" world of cyberspace,
extremes of climate attack the body in the form of flaming or being

frozen out of the conversation. Feminist/progressive contestation - claiming the public in cyberspace and constructing and reconstructing it through critical dialogue - has the potential to create a temperate, or hospitable climate that will provide life support for a participatory public space in both real and computer-mediated conversations.

Another important component of this climate work is the shift away from adversarial and competitive teaching and learning styles to a more cooperative style. The emphasis on climate as a factor in the learning process is directly connected to notions of a genuinely inclusive public sphere. Classrooms *are* public spaces and many educators have made the connections between increased learning opportunities for more of the students and the overall inclusivity of the environment, explicitly organizing classroom communities and modelling communicative virtues.

Feminists, too, having identified the historically exclusive structures of the public sphere and the relationship between masculinity and technology, have put this insight to use in modelling more inclusive alternatives. This modelling of inclusive practices can be applied as we create the public spaces fostered by new information technologies and can be used to provide a perspective from which to critically examine these new technologies and the spaces they influence.

A great deal of research and development has been dedicated to the creation of hardware and software that enables computer-based communication and the construction of on-line social spaces. My study of *ncf.general*, while non-exhaustive, provides some evidence that this aspect of the technology is insufficient for the expansion of truly public space, creating merely technically different social spaces, but not necessarily socially different spaces. In our search for inclusive public spaces, it continues to be the social technologies of public space, on- and off-line, that need attention. I have identified two appropriate loci for this attention: public education and feminist counterpublics.

Critical pedagogues and leaders in educational change movements are active in attempting to make classrooms more inclusive and to teach students how to enact public tendencies in other social spheres. These efforts need to be supported and broadened with critical engagement with and about new technologies embedded in them. The feminist tradition of creating more inclusive counterpublics, and the attention to gender and difference that have been key contributions of feminist and anti-racist scholarship need to be applied to any on-line activity.

In keeping with the intention of fostering technoliterate sceptics, the development of social technologies of the public needs to be attended to with a critical gaze. How do codes of conduct in discussion areas, for example, create new insiders and outsiders and to what extent is this intentional/desirable? How do efforts at broadening participation in classrooms undermine traditional bases of exclusion? How do they fail to undermine traditional bases of exclusion. Do they create new forms of marginalization? The title of Elizabeth Ellsworth's groundbreaking critique of early critical pedagogy is a healthy indication that these social technologies are being scrutinized: "Why Doesn't This Feel Empowering? Working Through the Repressive Myths of Critical Pedagogy".[4] This essay and others like it have been very effective in challenging some of the universalist assumptions of early critical pedagogy. Ellsworth's emphasis on the need to address difference meaningfully while deconstructing it has inspired successive efforts, such as the work of Burbules and Rice, to conceive of ways to be sensitive to difference and facilitate dialogue across difference. The "communicative virtues" developed by Burbules and Rice, I argue, are technologies of the public, and, like all technology, need to be approached with scepticism. But these technologies at least, are specifically aimed at creating greater inclusion. As such, they invite criticism, improvement and a celebration of possibility.

My identification of several model inclusive spaces was based on a brief exploration of the internet. Nonetheless, I was able to point to examples of inclusive spaces facilitated by detailed and thoughtful codes of conduct that attend to climate. These codes of conduct emphasize *freedom from* as opposed to *freedom to*. Questions for further research remain. To what extent are codes of conduct aimed at expanding inclusivity successful and how? How are sanctions applied? Do norms become arbitrary? Is *ncf.general* sufficiently representative of public spaces in cyberspace to provide evidence of exclusive tendencies? Would the public spaces I cite that model more inclusive tendencies through codes of conduct hold up to the same intensity of scrutiny? For example, would an in-depth analysis of conversations in Amazon City find that a less hostile quality of dialogue can be compatible with more subtle sexist and racist assumptions?

Just as Franklin draws our attention away from the typical focus of identifying what technology will enable to consider what technology will prevent, in our efforts to expand public space we need to be reflective in an ongoing way about the way in which our technologies of public space play out. How do codes of conduct expand inclusivity? Are new outsiders being created unintentionally? What kinds of conversations and expressions of perspective and identity might certain elements of codes of conduct prevent. What are the consequences of this prevention? Uneasiness about having the answers is a necessary consequence of postmodern reverence for complexity and multiple perspectives. Too many forms of oppression have resulted from righteousness and certainty. And yet, as with Haraway's assertion that the deconstruction of dualisms is a very political postmodernism, the querying of cyberspace in terms of inclusive and exclusive tendencies has implications for structures of power and inequality. Cyberspace is not set apart from society anymore than any other institution or medium.

The critique by feminists/postmodernists of the many dualisms contained and enacted within western culture suggests some guidelines for interacting with new technologies. Instead of perpetuating or enabling the illusion of the separation of body and mind, process and content, human and technological interfaces, Ullman's "code-switching" should be a guide. Multiple forms of communication should be fostered simultaneously. For example, intellectual activity should be combined with physical movement, solitary tasks should be structured around partnerships and joint responsibility, visual computer-based communication (text/symbols/images) should be combined with voice contact if not face to face interaction. Connections need to be made between interaction in cyberspace environments and other environments (the classroom, the mall, the family, the sports team, etceteras).

Research documenting feminist strategies for claiming public cyberspace is an emerging area within the literature and should be encouraged.[5] Feminist research to monitor the effectiveness of strategies aimed at inclusiveness, particularly in terms of unintended consequences, should be integral to feminist contestation of public cyberspace. For example, one of the questions that emerges with regard to the strategy of creating parallel feminist publics concerns the effect of ignoring hostile or polemic posts: does excluding others from "your" public space involve excluding yourself from "theirs" or from a more "common" public space? To what extent might inclusiveness be undermined by the very attempt to increase it? This may be, at least at times, an unintentional consequence of the establishment of parallel feminist publics.

In addition, research needs to be conducted with respect to the tensions between anonymity and safety, anonymity and textual violence, and anonymity and embodiment in cyberspace. There is no question that, for feminists and other marginalized groups contesting the climate in public cyberspace, the non-face-to-face character of the sight does provide some safety. At times this may be of considerable strategic value.

But at the same time, the anonymity in public cyberspaces that provides some measure of safety needs to be separated from the masculine cultures of both liberal democracy and computing that celebrate disembodiment. This is challenging because of the complexity of the issues involved. And, the measure of safety available in public cyberspaces needs to be understood as relative; after all, textual violence "really hurts" and has the effect of limiting participation. And, as mentioned above, the relationship between anonymity and the assumption of hegemonic norms of identity needs to be explored further. Ongoing feminist engagement with these and related questions is called for.

Ultimately, citizenship and entitlement to participation in public space needs to be conceived of in terms of rights *and* responsibilities. The public sphere, by definition, includes more than one person. If you do not seek ways to involve others, you can never claim to be in the public. This shift from emphasizing *freedom to* in public spaces to *freedom from* involves all participants in examining and reconstructing where appropriate the processes whereby boundaries are constructed and maintained between insiders and outsiders.

That is the argument of this book in a nutshell: cyberspace or not, unless public dispositions and skills are systematically taught/learned/modelled and actualized, exclusive practices will prevail.

NOTES

[1] J.B. Sykes, ed. *The Concise Oxford Dictionary of Current English.* (Oxford: Clarendon Press, 1976), p. 1188.

[2] J.B. Sykes, ed. *The Concise Oxford Dictionary of Current English.* (Oxford: Clarendon Press, 1976), p. 1188.

[3] Dale Spender, quoted in *White Noise: An A-Z of the Contradictions in Cyberculture.* (New York: St. Martin's Press, 1999, p.11.

[4] Elizabeth Ellsworth, "Why Doesn't This Feel Empowering? Working Through the Repressive Myths of Critical Pedagogy," in *Feminisms and Critical Pedagogy*, Carmen Luke and Jennifer Gore, eds. (New York: Routledge, 1992).

[5] Dale Spender, *Nattering on the Net: Women, Power and Cyberspace.* (Toronto: Garamond Press, 1995).

Index